BOYHOOD IN BEVERLEY

a mosaic of the 1920s

James Thirsk

Highgate of Beverley

Highgate Publications (Beverley) Limited

2003

British Library Cataloguing in Publication Data.
A catalogue record for this book is available from the British Library.

© 2003 James Thirsk

James Thirsk asserts the moral right to be identified as the author of this work.

ISBN 1 902645 37 5

Published by

Highgate of Beverley

Highgate Publications (Beverley) Limited
4 Newbegin, Beverley, HU17 8EG. Telephone (01482) 886017

Printed by Highgate Print Limited
4 Newbegin, Beverley, HU17 8EG. Telephone (01482) 886017

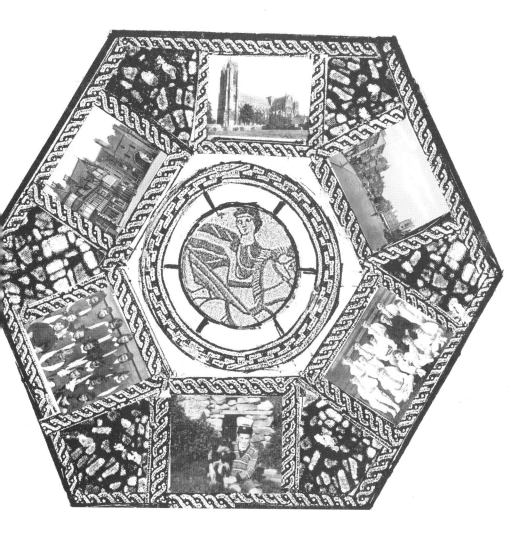

ACKNOWLEDGEMENTS

I wish to thank my sisters Jean Blackburn and Betty Thirsk, whose prodigious memories have helped me to tell this tale. Thanks also to my wife Joan, our daughter Jane Robinson and my cousin (once removed) Valerie Trueblood, all of whom read the manuscript, making valuable suggestions and corrections. My cousin, Roland Thirsk, (also once removed) I thank for ferreting out information from the Bridlington Library and from Beverley Grammar School. Our son, Martin Thirsk, guided me with unfailing patience when the computer refused to co-operate; for that help I thank him; also for scanning the photographs and transferring the manuscript on to disc. My thanks also to Dr John Markham and Mr Barry Sage for their help and advice with the manuscript. The closest of my old school friends, with whom I kept in touch for many years, are now dead; but how pleasing it has been to me to remember them in these pages.

Front cover: Saturday Market Place, Beverley, from a painting by Tom Burton in the Beverley Art Gallery. The date is 1920, and the scene is exactly how I remember it. My thanks to Patricia E Deans for the loan of the negative of this picture. Also to the Libraries and Information Department of the East Riding of Yorkshire Council for giving me permission to reproduce both this painting and the two photographs of Brid which are owned by the Bridlington Local Studies Library. I am grateful to Sandra Tichias for loan of the photograph of Miss Langley and Miss Spink.

CONTENTS

LETTER TO OUR GRANDCHILDREN

Dear Kate, Tim, James and Tom,

Do you remember that in my book, *A Beverley Child's Great War*, I wrote that I might one day tell you about my schooldays? Since then, I have been busy bringing to the light of day all those buried memories of boyhood, many of which have not surfaced for seventy and eighty years

It has been a happy task, because my life from six to sixteen, which coincided with the 1920s, was mostly a happy one, although, like all children, I had my share of disappointments.

Most of the sorrows of the world in that decade, in the aftermath of the Great War, passed me by; but, while I was busy with school and play, gigantic movements were changing the world, which affected everybody and led to the biggest economic depression ever seen, causing massive unemployment and poverty in many countries.

Why have I written of those days? Partly because I thought that you might be interested to hear what life was like inside and out of school all those years ago, at a time when there were no televisions, computers, pocket calculators, supermarkets, mobile phones, wireless sets (in our family), few telephones or motor-cars, little travel abroad (except for the wealthy) and no films with sound until the end of that decade – the list is endless.

Why are my memories of boyhood so vivid? The Danish novelist Martin Andersen Nexö, in his book, *Under the Open Sky: My Early Years*, explains it thus:

> Is there really anything so remarkable about remembering everything from childhood years as distinctly as though it had happened yesterday? Every experience was intensive then and was taken up by a mind that was bright and shiny and untouched, so that every contact left traces – often ineffaceable.

I was lucky to spend those years in the small market town of Beverley, across which you could cycle in a few minutes. It was so easy to see friends at their homes without travelling long distances on buses or trains and, above all, to have the freedom to roam on the Westwood. I wish you could all spend a few hours on the Westwood on a sunny summer's day. You would then realise why it meant so much to us. It is not really a wood; it is a vast expanse of undulating grassland, with woodland areas here and there.

The idea of telling my story in the form of a mosaic of small pieces came to me after reading a book by Valentin Kataev (1897-1986), who, in his eighties, wrote, *A Mosaic of Life: Memories of a Russian Childhood*. I hope that my mosaic will reveal a picture of a Yorkshire boy's life in the 1920s.

Perhaps one day you will all be writing about your childhood at the beginning of the 21st century; I hope they will be happy memories and that *your* grandchildren will enjoy hearing about them.

With love and best wishes from

Grandpa Jim Thirsk

THE HIGH SCHOOL FOR GIRLS

It is strange, I thought, that I cannot remember anything about my first day at school in 1919. You would think that such a momentous occasion would leave some trace on the memory. Yet trivial happenings come easily to the surface even after more than eighty years. For example, we had to remove our boots when arriving at school and don indoor shoes. One day during my first week at school, before going home for midday meal, I put my boots on the wrong feet. Aunt Annie was staying with us at the time and, as she saw me limping towards the house, she started laughing so much that the tears ran down her cheeks. 'Clara!,' she called to Mother, 'Charlie Chaplin's come home for his dinner.'

So I have to depend on my sister Jean's prodigious memory for more serious happenings. Although only three years older than I, she clearly remembers my first day at Beverley High School for Girls. As the hundred or so girls waited for the beginning of morning prayers, the Head Girl came from the Headmistress's room and through the door at the end of the hall. Hand in hand with five-year-old me, she walked to the front, depositing me on the floor with the other kindergarten children.

The hall I remember clearly with its highly polished wood floor, its wood-panelled walls and its tall pillars, which supported a gallery from which two classrooms led. I was to attend morning prayers in this hall for the next three years. The routine was always the same: while all the classes marched in and marked time, a senior girl played suitable music on the piano, such as *The British Grenadiers*. One of Jean's great friends, Evelyn Tero, was a brilliant pianist who regularly played the marching music. On the way to school Jean used to plead with her to play Sousa's stirring *Washington Post*, Jean's favourite. 'I can't play it every day,' said Evelyn. The teachers then arrived, ranging themselves in a row on the platform. Finally Miss D. C. Read, the English mistress who was also the Deputy Headmistress, came in to conduct proceedings. The girls sat on chairs but the youngest ones sat on the floor. Miss Gertrude Rossiter, the Headmistress, seldom appeared at prayers, but whether this was because she was shy or whether she believed in the delegation of duties we shall never know. After Miss Read, popularly known as DCR, had made necessary announcements, hymns were sung and prayers offered.

The school building was fairly new, for it was built in 1908, within the 12 acres belonging to Norwood House, a splendid Georgian dwelling. The old house was the residence of Miss Rossiter and some of the teachers, but it was also the home of the fee-paying boarders. The scholarship boarders, who did not pay fees, lived in a large house in Woodlands, away from the school. There life was more tolerable, supervised by Miss Fanny Rossiter, the Headmistresses's sister, who cared not so much for strict discipline.

The grounds consisted of smooth grassland big enough for two hockey-fields, surrounded by woods which were out of bounds. At one end, abutting the wooded area, was a lake with a little island in the middle, reached by a wooden bridge. The lake was said to be bottomless, the island haunted, and the bridge unsafe. Some of these tales were probably legends devised to prevent girls exploring and to keep them away from danger. Visits to the woods under supervision and on nature walks were permitted. Sometimes a moorhen and her chicks were seen on the lake, and sometimes a kingfisher. Tadpoles were collected for use in the biology class. But the woods were a great temptation, and my sister Jean remembers an adventure with two of her friends:

Three of us, Molly Mackrell, Christine Houlton and I were gardening one day after school hours on the small plot that was allocated to Form III. By 4 o'clock the last of the chattering schoolgirls had left, followed by the teachers, walking or on bicycles. We three worked on until we saw Mr Welburn, the caretaker, come out of his house and go into the school. As soon as the coast was clear, we climbed over the railings and were in the woods. Hiding our school-bags, we went deeper into the woods, which encircled the extensive playing-fields and one end of the lake. This was all forbidden territory and we were all laughing with excitement as we

The High School School Certificate class of 1926. Vera Hall: front row, second from the right. Jean Thirsk: top row, second from the left.

raced about, swinging on the branches of the trees. We even squeezed through a barrier and crossed the rickety old bridge across the lake to the little island in the middle. Returning to the woods we came to a little clearing. There to our horror we saw Miss Fanny Rossiter, the Art mistress, sister of the Headmistress, placidly seated at her easel, painting a woodland scene. We kept on running, hoping that she had not recognised us. Fortunately, she hadn't and there was no summons to the Head's presence the next morning.

We in the kindergarten were spared lessons from the legendary Mr Camidge, for Miss Langley, our teacher, had percussion instruments and we had lessons in eurythmics as she played the piano. From all accounts Mr Camidge was a man who caused some hilarity in the school. In addition to his job as the organist at Beverley Minster, he took all the music lessons at the High School and gave private piano lessons. Falstaffian in girth, he wore a monocle and purple socks. His bicycle was ancient, with a strange suspension system. His enormous weight made it difficult for him to mount the machine using the back step, so he propped the

The High School assembly hall.

3

bike against a wall and pushed himself off. In winter he wore a large cloak which billowed behind as he rode off. My sister Jean drew a picture of him pedalling away from the school with flying cloak. One of her friends, Lilian Peabody, who had private piano lessons, borrowed the picture, pretending that she wanted to show it to her parents. Instead she showed it to Mr Camidge. Later, in the playground, as she was talking to Jean, Mr Camidge walked by, wheeling his bicycle. 'Oh, Mr Camidge!,' cried Lilian, 'this is Jean, who drew the picture of you.' Jean was terribly embarrassed, but, to her surprise, Mr Camidge beamed, told her he liked it and said that he would like to keep it.

The High School, in its early years, had adopted the familiar Harrow School song, *Forty years on*, the words of which were not appropriate for a girls' school. Jean told me that some of them used to snigger at the words: *Visions of boyhood shall float them before you . . .*

During morning prayers at the beginning and end of term the appropriate half hymn was sung, composed by W. L. Viner (c.1856). with words by H. J. Buckoll (1803-1871):

> *Lord, behold us with thy blessing,*
> *Once again assembled here . . .*
> or
> *Lord dismiss us with thy blessing . . .*
> *Let this Father-hand be shielding*
> *All who here shall meet no more . . .*

At the end of the school year, when some of the older girls were leaving for the last time, they and their friends could be heard sobbing during the final verse.

Miss Gertrude Rossiter, the Headmistress, always presided over prayers on the first and last days of term. It was her custom on these occasions to read a verse from the *New Testament*, from Philippians, chapter 4, verse 8. Jean remembers 'the doom-laden voice with which she read the verse, her voice sinking lower and lower.'

> *Finally brethren, whatsoever things are true, whatsoever things are honest, whatsoever things are just, whatsoever things are pure, whatsoever things are lovely, whatsoever things are of good report; if there be any virtue, and if there be any praise, think on these things.*

THE KINDERGARTEN

When Friedrich Froebel came back to Berlin (c.1840), the idea of an institution for the education of little children had fully taken shape in his mind ... Long did he wrack his brains for a suitable name for his new scheme. Middendorff and I were one day walking to Blankenburg with him over the Steiger Pass. Froebel kept on repeating: 'Oh, if I could only think of a suitable name.'... Suddenly he stood still as if fettered fast to the spot ... Then he shouted to the mountains so that it echoed to the four winds of heaven: 'Eureka! I have it! Kindergarten (children's garden) shall be the name of the new institution!'

Johannes Arnold Barop (1802-1878)

In 1919, like many thousands of children after the Great War, I resented the return of a father whom I remembered vaguely from his visits home from France when wounded or on leave. The intrusion of this big man, who occupied so much of the house, was in my case aggravated by the arrival of a baby sister who took up so much of my mother's time. I still believed that my daddy 'in the France' was the one I preferred, and I wished that this daddy would go back to the France, taking the baby with him. Before I had time to get used to this new regime, I was told that in September I was to go to school for the first time to a mysterious place called a kindergarten.

Miss Langley, kindergarten mistress and Miss Spink (Botany teacher).

5

So here was I, one of only four boys in a class of fifteen, learning all kinds of new skills under the tuition of Miss Langley, a young woman who had undergone a Froebel training. Friedrich Froebel, (1781-1852), the nineteenth-century German educator, believed that his kindergarten should be a place where the teacher, the cultivator of the 'plants,' should encourage creativity and the development of inborn faculties. The teacher, rather than drilling the children, should foster self-expression through play, with music and poetry included in the games.

Miss Langley proved to be an excellent gardener, although she must have found the cultivation of her male plants difficult at times. The other three boys were Ken Annakin, an only child, who later in life became a film director; Gordon Armstrong, whose father at that time had invented a new kind of shock-absorber for cars and who had a motor repair business in North Bar Within. ('If Gordon Armstrong can't repair your car, scrap it!' was his slogan). Ronnie Chapman, was the fourth musketeer, but about him I remember nothing.

One of our activities was the art of plaiting. Some of the children were plaiting wool or raffia, but, in my case, Miss Langley suggested that I should plait the long hair of my neighbour in the classroom. Nancy Houlton, a farmer's daughter, obediently sat on a chair while I, sitting behind her, began to plait. Unhappily a devil-imp put the idea

The Kindergarten, 1921.
Top row: Dora Maw, Ken Annakin, --?, --?, Gordon Armstrong, Evelyn Duggleby.
Middle Row: Olive Turgoose, Kathleen Bremner, Joan Maxwell, Enid Bursell, --?
Bottom Row: Ron Chapman, Cynthia Dobson, Nancy Houlton, Jimmy Thirsk.

into my head that I should plait her hair, interweaving it into the framework of the wooden chair. Nancy was not amused, but I cannot remember that Miss Langley was angry. What would old Froebel have said? In the only photograph of the kindergarten children that I have, Nancy is sitting next to me with her ears covered by her hands. Had I said something which she refused to hear? At the end of the first term Miss Langley wrote in my school report, under the heading *General conduct*: 'Jimmy is rough with the girls.' Now I have no memory of being rough with anybody; however, the record was there for all to see. Perhaps my plaiting exercise was thought to be rough on Nancy Houlton.

Miss Langley believed in the virtues of eurhythmics; while she played the piano we all attempted to harmonise our movements. One trick I learnt, which I can still perform, was beating time up and down with the left hand and at the same time beating down, across and up with the right hand, as if tracing the outline of a triangle. This is a feat which many people find impossible.

At morning prayers the kindergarten pupils all sat on the floor in front of the Deputy Headmistress. We four boys were lost in what seemed to us a multitude of girls of all shapes, sizes and ages, although, in fact, the total number in the school was little more than one hundred.

After two years in the kindergarten we all moved into the first form, where Miss Dearden took charge of us. There, with stricter discipline, although I remember that Miss Dearden was a kind teacher, we began to do sums and write. These were very different activities from those we had enjoyed in the kindergarten.

The year in the first form completed my days at Beverley High School. Three years of what now seems to have been a dream-like life had ended. After the usual holiday at Bridlington, in September 1922, I was to plunge into the battlefield of Beverley Grammar School, cowed by the unaccustomed playground rowdiness of about one hundred and fifty boys.

THE SNEEZE

In the ordinary course of life a sneeze is of no great importance. You sneeze. Somebody says 'Bless you!' and life goes on. However, my sneeze, before morning prayers at Beverley High School one day in 1920, had disastrous consequences.

The kindergarten class had filed into the school hall for morning prayers. The rest of the school, probably about one hundred girls of all shapes and sizes, filled the remainder of the hall. Just as we were all assembled that morning and as we waited for the Deputy Headmistress to appear, I sneezed. It was a tremendous sneeze for one so small and what was unfortunate was that I had a nasty cold and no handkerchief.

Miss Langley, our kindergarten mistress, came to a rapid decision. Not having any tissues, which at that time had not been invented, she said: 'Go to the classroom, Jimmy, and wait there until the end of prayers.' Ashamed, and no doubt followed by the titters of the whole class, I hastily left the hall.

Miss Langley hadn't time to suggest any task that I should do in the classroom. So, having looked around the room, I sat for a while listening to the distant sound of the school singing hymns, to the accompaniment of a piano played by one of the senior girls.

And it was then that the chapter of accidents began. Noticing a vase of flowers on the top of a low cupboard, I reached up to lift it down so that I could smell the flowers. Alas! The flowers tipped out on to the floor. The vase, which was not broken, I hastily put back with the flowers in it; but most of the water lay in a large puddle on the polished wooden floor of the classroom. What could I do? There were no floor cloths. I decided that the only way to hide the puddle of water was to soak it up in the jersey I was wearing. But instead of taking off my jersey, I lay face downwards on the floor, mopping up the water by swimming in it.

Miss Langley must have noticed my damp condition as soon as she returned with the children. 'What on earth have you done, Jimmy?' she asked. 'I was trying to smell the flowers,' I said tearfully, 'and all the water fell out on the floor.'

My sister Jean remembers what happened next. Miss Langley appeared in Form III, walking up to the form mistress, Miss Allen, with whom she held a whispered conversation, with both of them smiling broadly. 'Jean,' said Miss Allen, 'will you please go with Miss Langley to the kindergarten?' Mystified, Jean went along with Miss Langley, who explained on the way what had happened. 'Will your mother be at home?' she asked. 'I think so,' said Jean. 'Then could you please take Jimmy home at once? You can bring him back to school after lunch when he is clean and dry.'

THE LIE DIRECT

We four seven-year-old boys, still heavily outnumbered by the girls, had moved up to the first form after our two years in the kindergarten at Beverley High School for Girls. It was to be our final year at this school, for boys were not allowed to progress beyond the first form. Miss Dearden, the form mistress, looked after us like a mother-hen; she was a gentle soul who never, to my recollection, lost her temper, although she must have often been tempted to do so.

The girls had their own toilet somewhere in the building, but we boys had a special one. If you walked through the hall where morning prayers took place, you came to a corridor with rooms leading off. One of these was the Headmistress's room. To the left another door revealed a book-room, where many shelves of new school textbooks were stored before distribution to the classes. Walking through this room with its pleasant smell of new books, you came to another door leading to a single toilet. Miss Dearden lined us four boys up at the entrance to the big hall each day after a morning break, sending us one by one to the toilet.

One morning, coming back through the book room, I noticed on a table an ink-pad and a rubber-stamp. I was always interested in printing, for by that time I had my first John Bull printing set, a present which gave me great pleasure, arranging small pieces of rubber type to form a sentence. I looked for a piece of paper on which to try out the rubber-stamp. There was none. Above the table however, devoid of shelves, a clean expanse of white-painted wall caught my eye. Without any thought of consequences I inked the rubber stamp on the pad and pressed the words BEVERLEY HIGH SCHOOL in the middle of the wall. Had I had any sense I would have stamped one of the new books which were waiting to be stamped anyway.

Nobody can have noticed my crime for several days, but one day Miss Dearden asked each of us boys separately if we knew anything about the lettering on the wall. I said 'No, Miss Dearden.' It was the first time that I ever remember lying. Minor lies we called fibbing in those days, which did not sound as serious. But this was a LIE DIRECT; the other boys denied of course that they had done it.

I wonder now whether Miss Dearden had a good idea who was the culprit, from the way we answered. Nobody was punished and my secret has been hidden from the world for eighty years. I still remember clearly the satisfaction I enjoyed when I made my mark on that spacious clean wall. It is probably still there under many layers of emulsion paint.

FIRST LOVE AND A SILVER BOOT

We that are true lovers run into strange capers.

As You Like It

It happened one morning during my first week at Beverley Grammar School in the autumn of 1922. Those were exciting times: we had just returned from a family holiday in Bridlington, my first bicycle had arrived, I was eight years old, and here was I cycling along Lairgate, my only apprehension the unknown perils of a new school.

Suddenly I saw coming towards me on the pavement a beautiful young girl. Obviously she was on her way to school, for she wore the bright blue pleated tunic, the summer dress of the pupils of Beverley High School for Girls. My glimpse of her was for two seconds only as I pedalled by, but it was long enough for me to fall in love with this dark–haired girl with sparkling brown eyes and of breathtaking beauty.

As each morning came I watched eagerly for her appearance, sometimes alone, sometimes with a fellow pupil. I began to time my journey to school so that I would pass her at the same place in Lairgate. What rapture when she began to notice me and smile! Too timid to jump off my bike and speak to her, I decided that I would write a letter which, although written from the heart, I fear had much nonsense in it. Although I cannot remember the words, I am sure that it contained a declaration of my love. I folded the letter several times and threw it on the pavement a few yards ahead of her. She had seen me do this, and as I turned in my saddle I saw her pick it up.

Although I did not know her name, I must have signed my own name in full. For when she read the surname she would have guessed that I was the brother of Jean Thirsk, one of her eleven-year-old classmates. No reply came to my letter but she smiled and waved every morning as I rode by, gladdening my heart.

My sister Jean told me that her name was Vera Hall and that Vera had shown my letter to her. Jean teased me about it, but told me that Vera was amused and touched by my declaration of love. This one-sided love affair continued and I penned more little notes declaring my adoration. Wishing to give Vera some token of my devotion I enclosed with my next note a little silver boot. Where this came from I do not know; it was not real silver of course and may have come from a Christmas cracker. Perhaps a red rose would have been a better token. But how was I to know?

How the affair came to an end I do not now remember. Perhaps Vera found another way to school? Or perhaps, a year older, I cycled past her too embarrassed to look?

BEVERLEY GRAMMAR SCHOOL

It was sixty or seventy years after I left Beverley Grammar School in 1930 that I walked up the familiar Queensgate to see what changes there had been. As I passed the old building I saw for the first time the complex of buildings which now occupy part of our old playing-fields. It was as if a genie out of the *Thousand and one Nights* had suddenly planted all those buildings overnight.

How often must Mr Burden, our Headmaster, have dreamed of such a school. The old school, as I remember it when I first saw it in 1922, consisted of the main brick building beyond the cemetery, and two wooden huts nearby, each containing three classrooms that had been added to cope with the larger number of boys. This had risen from about seventy, when the school was built in 1902, to about one hundred and thirty in 1922.

The school had come to rest at the top of Queensgate after occupying several sites in Beverley since medieval days. Founded probably in pre-Conquest times and perhaps the oldest Grammar School in England, it was always closely connected with the Minster. The first school, built in the south-west corner of the churchyard, was demolished and rebuilt there in 1606-1608.

Celia Fiennes (1662-1741), that intrepid horsewoman, whose, *Through England on a Side Saddle in the time of William and Mary,* first appeared in 1888, included in her description of Beverley a mention of the Grammar School:

The old Grammar School in the Minster churchyard (from Poulson's Beverlac 1829).

There is a very good free schoole for boys, they say the best in England for learning and care, which makes it fill'd with Gentlemens sons besides the free schollars from all parts.

Daniel Defoe, in his *A Tour through England and Wales*, the first volume of which appeared in 1724, also mentions that Beverley has:

A free-school that is improved by two fellowships, six scholarships, and three exhibitions in St John's College, in Cambridge, belonging to it.

After more than two centuries a new school was built in Keldgate. Yet another move came, to Albert Terrace, before the move to Queensgate.

In the main building were two central class-rooms divided by a rolling partition. They served as an assembly hall each morning, when about one hundred and thirty boys filed in, followed by the staff who stood at the front. Tattersall, a boy in my class, was chosen to go to the staff room next door to summon the masters. Willie Burrow, our English master, called him the *muezzin*, calling the faithful to prayer. After assembly the partition was rolled down so that the 5th and 5th

First Form, c.1923.
Standing: John Huzzard, Bradley, Mike Burton, Geoff Thirsk, Clapham.
Seated: Ken Annakin, Richardson, Mrs. Watson (teacher), Mr. Burden (headmaster), Wetherby, Andrews. Front row: Dixon, Jimmy Thirsk, Ironside (Tinribs), Straker.

12

Form Upper could occupy separate rooms. In the 5th form by the window hung the rope to toll the school bell on the wall outside. As well as the staff room, a music room stood on the opposite side of the corridor. Further along the corridor was the Headmaster's study.

On my first day at school that morning in September 1922, I was taken with Ken Annakin, both of us eight years old, to see the Headmaster in his study. Charles Henry Burden, known by all the boys as 'Paddy,' greeted us and asked us to wait there until after morning assembly. While we waited we could hear the singing of hymns and the Headmaster's voice raised in prayer. We saw the books which covered the whole of one wall; we also noticed several canes in an upright cylinder by the fireplace. When Paddy returned he welcomed us to the school and, after gently telling us that we must always behave in a way which would not bring dishonour to the school, sent us on our way to Form I classroom. Before many days had passed we lost our timidity. Standing with our class on the front row at morning assembly, we were soon singing the hymns as lustily as the other boys.

Next door to Paddy's study Mr Cross, an Oxford graduate, ruled over the chemistry laboratory. Later we found that Mr Cross's way of controlling a class was to walk around the room holding a length of rubber tubing which he swung through the air until it whistled. Sometimes, if we had a chemistry lesson immediately after morning assembly, Mr Cross would be called away for a few minutes to witness a caning in Paddy's study. He returned to the lab. smiling sadistically. We did not dare ask him how many canings on each hand had been administered.

The only other room in the main building was the Physics laboratory. Here ruled Old Bill Williams, the deputy head, surrounded by Nicholson's hydrometers, Wheatstone Bridges and other apparatus. A genial Welshman, he, like Paddy, had an unusual combination of degrees, being a B.A. and B.Sc. (London and Wales), with a 1st class honours degree in mathematics.

The hut nearest the school building housed the sixth-form at one end and the first form at the other. The other hut, built on stilts, housed the art room at one end and classes III and IV. At the end of the corridor which ran the whole length of the hut was a small locked room full of equipment used by the Cadet Force. In this corridor Ken Annakin and I stood one morning in our first week, waiting presumably with sixty or seventy other boys for the summons to assembly. I was alarmed by the deafening cries and shouts of the temporarily unleashed boys. One of them was blowing blasts on a bugle which he must have taken from the Cadet Force room. It was all very frightening for two small boys, more used to the gentler way of life at the girls' High School.

Sometimes the doors and window in the huts, not able to cope with damp conditions, caused problems, unlike the sash windows in the main building. One door nearly caused the death of a master. Flemmy Rogers, the history teacher, was in charge of the 1st Form one day when a boy asked if he could leave the room; but, finding he could not open the outer door, he came back and told Mr Rogers, who also tried to open the door without success. Johnny Huzzard then volunteered to climb out through a window so that he could open the door from the outside. Finding it still stuck he raised his foot and gave the door a powerful kick with his boot. Unknown to him, Mr Rogers was still trying the door from the inside. The door flew open, hitting Flemmy a tremendous blow on the forehead. He fell to the ground groaning. We all thought for a few moments that he was dead.

We had no gymnasium in which we could practise. If the weather was fine our P.T. (Physical Training) classes were outside in the grounds. When it rained a master would take the class into the long cycle-shed off Sloe Lane, there to hang from ladders stretched across the rafters.

Outside the main building was the playground, a rectangular space. At the end was another cycle-shed and beyond that were expanses of grassland about the size of three football pitches. A couple of years before I left the school in 1930, a new sports pavilion was built, equipped with changing rooms and showers with hot and cold water. It was a memorial to the boys of the school who had died in the Great War.

The premises were far too small for a school with a growing population. Paddy Burden's dream of a new school in place of the inadequate buildings of the 1920s and early thirties was not realised until 1936 when a new brick building was opened. By that time he had retired; but he came to the opening ceremony as Mayor of Beverley.

BEVERLEY

Born in Hull I cannot call myself a true Beverlonian, which name only those born in Beverley are entitled to use. However, they say that it's an ill wind that blows nobody any good. In my case the ill winds were the Zeppelin raids in the early days of the Great War, which persuaded Mother to leave her house in Hull and return to Beverley where her mother, father and several sisters lived. Dad, away in the army already, hearing of the raids on Hull, had urged her to find a house to rent in Beverley. So it happened that I became a citizen of Beverley at the age of one, with my elder brother David aged six and sister Jean age four.

*The North Bar,
from without.*

*The North Bar,
from within.*

The poet Eric Chilman must have been a Beverlonian, or, if not, he had lived in Beverley long enough to love the town. Here is his poem, *Beverley*:

I know a town where music dwells
In plangent psalmody of bells,
And men keep whole from ages gone
The grey-gold Minster of St John.

The folk of town and countryside
By North Bar and St Mary's ride,
And farmers talk of gain and loss
Beside a Georgian market cross.

In March the wold-winds reel and spin
Down Westwood slope to Newbegin
The thorn-trees hold their Maytide state,
And rooks in elm-trees congregate.

I know a town so comely seen
In Gothic glory ringed with green.
A man might sing in that keen air
His nunc dimittis, *praising her.*

I have heard strangers say how much they enjoyed their first visit to Beverley. When you stand in Saturday Market Place and gaze around you have the feeling that this town has been there forever. There are in fact few medieval buildings, apart from the Minster and St Mary's Church, but in some curious way you are aware of a thousand years of history. Few strangers coming to Beverley know that in medieval times it was a thriving town, greater in population than Hull, with its own outlet to the North Sea via Beverley Beck, the River Hull and the Humber. The layout of the town is irregular and some of the streets have unusual names such as Lairgate, Newbegin, Flemingate and Dog and Duck Lane. All the old gates to the town have gone except the North Bar, a medieval brick building which has defied the modern world. To permit the passage of double-decker buses they had to be specially shaped to allow them to go through. The two streets on either side are known as North Bar Within and North Bar Without. Beverley was never a walled town, but there was a ditch and five gates.

One painting in the Beverley Art Gallery captures for me the essence of Beverley. Tom Burton, a local artist of some renown, painted this picture in 1920. The scene shows the northern end of the market place on a dark snowy Saturday night, with St Mary's Church in the background. To the right are the stall-holders ranged alongside

The Market Place looking towards St. Mary's Church.

The Market Place, Beverley.

Butter Ding Flags, their wares lit up by naphtha flares. This scene had changed little in the 1920s when I remember it.

Most people who have lived in Beverley and have foolishly gone away, long to go back. If they cannot, they long to visit the town again. The chimes of Beverley Minster are familiar to all Beverlonians and are probably heard in dreams all over the world. The best view of Beverley for the exile returning is seen as you descend through the Westwood on the York Road; across the rolling grassland you see the Black Mill, a lone sentinel shorn of its sails. In front you see the towers of the Minster and St Mary's Church.

Celia Fiennes in the 1690s and Daniel Defoe in the 1720s, travelling to Beverley along this road, also saw this memorable view of the town. Celia saw the Westwood when it was much more wooded than now.

Beverley, she wrote, *is a very fine town ... the Market Cross is large; there are three markets one for Beasts, another for Corne and another for fish, all large. The town is serv'd with water, by wells walled up round or rather in a Square, above halfe ones length, and by a pully and weight let down or draws up the bucket which is chained to the beame of the pully. There are many of these wells in all the streetes, it seemes its in imitation of Holland, they being supply'd with water soe. The buildings are new and pretty ...*

Celia was more interested in food, drink and places than in people but it is good to know that the Beverley tradesmen served her well:

Provision being very cheape, I was offered a large codffish for a shilling and good Pearch very cheape, we had Crabbs bigger than my two hands, pence apiece, which would have cost 6 pence if not a shilling in London, and they were very sweete.

Daniel Defoe also gave a favourable account of Beverley:

It is above a mile in length, being of late much improv'd in its buildings, and has pleasant springs running through its streets. It is more especially beautiful with two stately churches ... The principal trade of the town is making malt, oatmeal and tann'd leather, but the poor people mostly support themselves by working bone-lace.

Referring to the privilege of sanctuary, Defoe mentions the stone sanctuary chair in the Minster:

It is easy to conceive, he says, *how Beverley became a town from this very article, namely that all the thieves, murtherers, housebreakers and bankrupts, fled hither to protection; and here they obtained safety from the law whatever their crimes might be.*

Although not mentioning the Westwood, Defoe writes of a spaw (spa)*:*

> *About a mile from Beverley to the east, in a pasture belonging to the town, is a kind of spaw, though they say it cannot be judg'd by the taste whether or no it comes from any mineral; yet taken inwardly it is a great drier, and wash'd in, dries scorbutick scurf, and all sorts of scabs, and also very much helps the King's evil.*

The plan of central Beverley is so clearly imprinted on my brain that I can still imagine cycling through those familiar streets; in truth, if ghosts exist, of people and bicycles, I shall probably be seen there many years hence. It is true that there have been changes over the years; but these are only superficial in the centre of the town and they do not shock me whenever I return. As I stand in the Market Place I have this feeling, shared, I am sure, by many, that Beverley is part of me. To walk through it, or in any of the familiar streets or on the Westwood, always makes me think that it all belongs to me.

When I was six years old I walked one day along St Mary's Terrace, down Newbegin, through Newbegin Passage and along the market place to Toll Gavel, where my cousin Geoff lived. A neighbour spotted me and later told Mother that, as I walked along Toll Gavel, I was singing at the top of my voice a song which had only come out a couple of years before. 'You would have thought that he owned the town,' she said.

> *I'm forever blowing bubbles,*
> *Pretty bubbles in the air,*
> *They fly so high,*
> *Nearly reach the sky,*
> *Then like my dreams*
> *They fade and die.*
> *Fortune's always hiding,*
> *I've looked everywhere,*
> *I'm forever blowing bubbles,*
> *Pretty bubbles in the air.*

WIRELESS

They used to talk about wireless telegraphy and wireless telephony in the early 1890s, but it was not until after the Great War, in the 1920s, that the word 'wireless' was used to mean a radio receiver. It was then that the man in the street was able to buy or make himself a simple wireless receiver, known as a crystal set.

These early wireless sets enabled the listener to pick up, using head-phones, the few broadcasts then existing; he could also listen to many messages in the Morse code, most of them from merchant ships. A fine metal wire, called the 'cat's whisker,' when scratched across the surface of a semi-conducting crystal, produced the sounds of music or speech. The wireless sets using valves and loudspeakers came on the market later in the 1920s.

In the first form at Beverley Grammar School, one of my close friends was Johnny Huzzard, the son of a farmer at Bishop Burton, about three miles from Beverley. Johnny cycled down to school and sometimes I went back with him to play on the farm, have tea there and cycle home. Johnny was bitten by the craze for making crystal sets. After school he bought with his pocket money the necessary parts from a shop in the Market Place at Beverley. After several weeks he had everything he wanted and had completed his crystal set.

There remained one important item. If you wanted to achieve good reception, you required a good aerial. Most people, including my father, bought a long pole which was inserted in the ground, usually at the end of the garden. From the top of the pole a wire led to the top floor of the house, then down inside the house to the crystal set. At the farm there was no need to use a pole, for the Huzzard's farm and outbuildings were high. Johnny and I climbed up on the roof of the farmhouse to fix one end of the aerial there; the other end was attached to the barn. After such strenuous work we were ready for a sumptuous tea, which included chopped bananas, smothered with sugar and the thickest cream I ever remember eating. Mrs Huzzard knew what boys liked. One day, after tea, the heaviest downpour of rain I had ever seen, made me wonder how I would get home. Johnny's father, the farmer, came to my rescue by putting my bike in the back of a farm truck and driving me home to Beverley snug and warm in the front with him.

All the fun was in the making of the crystal set and in trying to find programmes by applying the cat's whisker to the crystal. I cannot remember sitting for long listening to a programme. The magic was that we could pick up from the outside world scraps of music and talk and the ever-present Morse code signals. To us it was amazing that all around us were these wireless waves which could only be heard through a wireless set.

It wasn't long before crystal sets were superseded by valve sets which broadcast through a loudspeaker to everybody within earshot. At this stage Dad refused to have one, believing that it would distract us children from our homework. It was not until September 1938 that he rented a powerful radio at the time of the Munich crisis, when many believed that war was imminent; but by that time we four children had all left home.

At the age of eleven Johnny Huzzard left the Grammar School to go to a boarding-school and I never saw him again.

PADDY BURDEN THE HEADMASTER

Had our Headmaster at Beverley Grammar School been six feet tall instead of about five feet six inches he would have been a fearful figure indeed. His large head and craggy features would have looked better on a taller man. However, in spite of his lack of height, he was to us boys a person whom we feared and respected most of the time.

Charles Henry Burden, or 'Paddy,' as he was always known by the boys, had unusual qualifications; he was a Bachelor of Science and a Bachelor of Arts. How this came about we did not know; but there were rumours that he had been an engineer and had studied privately for both these University of London degrees.

Mathematics, which included arithmetic, algebra, geometry and trigonometry, was his special subject. There was no separate teacher of mathematics because Paddy himself conducted classes in that subject at every level. He was able to draw a perfect circle on the blackboard freehand; this feat always caused the class to give a muted cheer, which obviously pleased him.

Paddy was also proficient in French and Latin and, although Greek was not taught at school, he often betrayed some knowledge of that language. One of his firm beliefs was that we should always know the origin of the words we use. If a word like *homogeneous* cropped up during a lesson, he would pause, write the word on the blackboard and ask us if we knew the etymology. When nobody spoke, he explained that the ancient Greek word *homos* meant 'the same' and *genos* meant 'kin.' Another example was the word *obstreperous,* meaning noisy or clamorous. This he told us was from the Latin: *ob* meaning against and *strepere,* to rattle or make a noise.

One of Paddy's anecdotes (and there were many), which I never forgot, was his explanation of the phrase: 'Let's go back to our muttons,' which sometimes people say when they want to bring an argument back to the subject. Paddy told us that in an old French play: *L'avocat Patelin,* by Abbé David-Augustin de Brueys, a cloth-dealer was prosecuting his shepherd for stealing some sheep. When a lawyer is questioning him, his mind keeps wandering to other matters. The judge tries to bring him back to his story by imploring him: *Revenons à ces moutons!* (Let's return to these sheep!)

Paddy had come to Beverley Grammar School as Headmaster in 1912, a couple of years before the Great War, in which he served as a special constable. One dark night he had been patrolling the town in pitch darkness. Knowing that there were some iron railings somewhere ahead, he extended his arms in front of him. Unfortunately his arms passed between the railings bringing his nose in sharp contact with the middle rail. 'In similar circumstances,' he warned us, 'make sure that you clasp your hands together before extending your arms in front.'

As the Great War progressed, with more and more Beverley boys in the casualty lists, he grieved at the loss of so many of them who had attended the school and whom he knew so well. After the war he became an active proponent of the League of Nations, speaking at many meetings in the town. He also sponsored the attendance of several German boys at the Grammar School in the 1920s.

Then came the Second World War. He had retired by then but many more old boys of the Grammar School were listed as dead or missing. The school was small enough for him to remember most of the boys who had been there in his time. When my brother David was reported missing, and later killed, Paddy wrote a moving letter of condolence to my parents, declaring that: 'We can ill afford to lose such men.'

After more than a thousand morning assemblies conducted by Paddy, every boy became so familiar with his voice, his walk, his angers and benevolent smiles, that we knew him better than we knew our fathers. We learned how to laugh at his jokes and to murmur our sympathy when he spoke of sad things. In all this time we must have sung all the hymns in *Hymns Ancient and Modern* several times over. The dreaded moment came at the end of morning assembly when we heard these words: 'I wish to see Oliver, Pottage, Skinner and Thirsk minor in my study at the close of assembly.' This was the time when hearts missed beats as the named boys racked their brains trying to think which rule they had transgressed.

Paddy was a nonconformist and a member of the Wesleyan chapel in Toll Gavel. On Founder's Day, however, because of the school's close association with Beverley Minster from medieval times, the whole school marched down to attend a special service there.

Paddy was always adamant that the school rules must never be disobeyed. At the beginning of each school year he stressed the importance of good manners. So concerned was he about the reputation of the school in Beverley and further afield that he warned us to remove our school cap if ever we were tempted to engage in disreputable pursuits.

He was a just man, but intolerant of wickedness and deceit. In his study several thin canes stood in a container close to his desk. Caning, always on the hands, was a last resort and it was never given for trivial offences and never administered by any other master. The very sight of the canes when you entered his study was enough to persuade you not to stray from the path of righteousness.

He was not a great sportsman, although he was a great advocate of Juvenal's proposal: *Mens sana in corpore sano* (A sound mind in a sound body). I remember him playing cricket only once in a parents versus teachers match at the Norwood cricket ground. Fielding the ball near the boundary, Paddy threw it with such accuracy and velocity that the stumps flew in all directions and the batsman was run out. The spectators roared their approval and it was obvious that Paddy was pleased with his prowess.

Sometimes we wondered that, like Oliver Goldsmith's village schoolmaster, 'one small head could carry all he knew.' He retired in 1934 after twenty-two years as Headmaster. From 1936 to 1938 he was Mayor of Beverley; in that capacity he attended the opening of the new school building which had been his dream for so long.

Paddy married twice. A son by his first wife was I.C.J. Burden. The son of his second marriage, Donald Burden, was a bearded sailor in the Navy in World War II. Both had attended the Grammar School. A daughter Mary went to Beverley High School. Paddy Burden died in his ninetieth year, in 1957.

Requiescat in pace!

THE SCHOOL MOTTO

Every boy who was at Beverley Grammar School knew by heart the four words of the school motto: *Adolescentiam alunt, senectutem oblectant*. We were told that it referred to books and literature, which *nourish youth and are the solace of old age*. Although we all knew the meaning, nobody told us where it came from or when it had been adopted by the school. Perhaps neither the Latin master nor the Headmaster knew.

By chance, many years after leaving school, I came across the words in one of the speeches of the Roman orator, Marcus Tullius Cicero (106-43 B.C.); he was pleading in court the case of the Greek poet Archias of Antioch, who was accused of assuming Roman citizenship illegally. In his speech Cicero spoke of the poetry of Archias and of the many virtues of literature:

> *Other pursuits, he said, belong not to all times, all ages, all conditions; but this gives <u>stimulus to our youth and diversion to our old age</u> ; this adds a charm to success, and offers a haven of consolation to failure. In the home it delights, in the world it hampers not. Through the night watches, on all our journeyings, and in our hours of country ease, it is an unfailing companion.*

This translation of the passage from Cicero's speech is from the Loeb edition, whose editor writes of it in these words:

> *This speech* Pro Archia poeta, *contains what is perhaps the finest panegyric of literature that the ancient world offers us: a panegyric which has been quoted and admired by a long series of writers from Quintilian, through Petrarch, until today, when it has lost none of its lustre; and which perhaps inspired a great Elizabethan scholar and gentleman, Sir Philip Sidney, in his* An Apologie for Poetrie (1595), *to write of poetry that* It holdeth children from play and old men from the chimney-corner.

Cicero won his case and Archias became a Roman citizen, taking the name Aulus Licinius Archias. In later years Cicero fell on evil times. He was a republican who, although he opposed Julius Caesar, was not invited to take part in the conspiracy to assassinate him. His own death came within a year of Caesar's. Three men, Antonius, Octavian and Lapidus, bent on seizing power, met on an island in the river Rhenus, near Bologna. It was here that they appointed themselves a triumvirate, with absolute power for five years. One of their first tasks was to condemn to death many of their opponents, including Cicero. He was murdered by soldiers in the neighbourhood of his villa at Formiae. His head and severed hands were displayed in Rome.

Plutarch, in his essay on Cicero tells of his brilliant schooldays:

> *For as soon as he was of an age to begin to have lessons, he became so distinguished for his talent, and got such a name and reputation amongst the boys, that their fathers would often visit the school that they might see young Cicero and might say that they themselves had witnessed the quickness and readiness in learning for which he was renowned.*

Plutarch does not say what Cicero's fellow class-mates thought about this. I wonder what the Latin was for 'beastly swot.'

THE SIX-SHOOTER

My school friends wouldn't believe me when I told them that my Dad had a revolver, a real six-shooter that he had kept when he came out of the army in 1919. We were all about twelve years old at the time.

One boy, from another class, had brought to school a starting pistol, which looked like the real thing. 'Somebody has drilled out the solid metal of the barrel,' he said, 'and if I could get some bullets it would fire.' He showed us this treasure furtively during morning break, for if Paddy Burden, the Headmaster, had heard about this there would have been serious trouble and a caning, probably six on each hand, which was the maximum punishment. 'My Dad has a small tobacco tin with bullets in it which fit his revolver,' I said. They still didn't believe me.

One day that summer, in the school holidays, three of my friends had cycled to our house in Norwood to play in the garden. Mother had gone out, so here was my opportunity. Creeping upstairs with my friends, I opened a big tin trunk, which stood on the middle landing. Penetrating to the bottom through layers of blankets and unused winter clothes, I brought out a heavy service revolver in a holster – a six-shooter – and a box with a few rounds of ammunition. They were all amazed and one of them dared me to load it and fire it in the garden. Fortunately I didn't. They all handled it and admired this powerful weapon. Now they believed me. Replacing it in the trunk, we returned to our play in the garden.

Dad never found out at the time, but I remember telling him about the escapade many years later during the Second World War. How careless he was to have stored it in an unlocked trunk! There it lay for many years until one day only a couple of years before the war Dad heard of a general amnesty for weapons. Because there had been terrorist bombs in London and other towns it was decreed that anybody who handed to the police weapons of any kind would not have to explain possession of them or have their names taken. Dad walked down one evening to the Beverley police station, handing in his revolver and ammunition.

Two years later the Second World War came. In 1940, hearing the broadcast appeal for men to join a citizens' army, Dad enrolled in the Local Defence Volunteers (L.D.V.) which was later renamed the Home Guard. At first they were desperately short of weapons of all kinds and Dad bitterly regretted that his old revolver was not still in the tin trunk.

MY DOUBLE COUSIN GEOFF

My cousin Geoff, slightly over one year older than me, was a double first cousin. Two of the Thirsk brothers, my father and his brother Jim, both Beverlonians, but brought up in Scotland, married two of the many daughters of Henry and Damaris Lydia Chapman of Beverley. Geoff had two older brothers and two older sisters; I had an older brother, one older sister and one younger sister.

In between the ages of five and eleven, just after the Great War, Geoff and I were inseparable companions. Bernard, Geoff's oldest brother, christened us Mutt and Jeff, after the American cartoon characters. We were not a bit alike in character. Geoff was much slower than I, always thinking before he took action. He had poor eyesight, which meant that he always wore spectacles.

He began attending Beverley Grammar School at the age of nine and was in the same class as I was all the way through school. He was known as Thirsk minor, my brother being Thirsk major; I came last as Thirsk tertius. At games Geoff never shone. His eyesight inhibited him at cricket and football. I enjoyed cricket and, though not much use as a batsman, I was not a bad bowler. Football I enjoyed also if the weather was good.

Geoff was not a scholar. He had come to the Grammar School from a small private school in Beverley, run by an elderly lady. He never came anywhere near the top of the class; in fact almost every week he was in the bottom third of our class of about thirty boys. At the end of each term we were given a sealed report to take home to our parents. One term-end Geoff's mother opened his report, read the gloomy news and said: 'Oh Geoff, why can't you be like Jim and get good marks?' Geoff hotly replied: 'I work harder than him. Our Jim's clever, but by gum, he is lazy!' It was true: I loved mathematics, French and English, but had no great interest in chemistry, physics and the other subjects. My position in class was usually around the middle.

Geoff and I spent a lot of time together during the school holidays. His dad, my Uncle Jim, was the manager of the Beverley Gasworks and also of the Waterworks. We often played in the grounds of the Gasworks. The clerk in the weighbridge office used to let us use his typewriter, which was a great thrill for me. This was where the loads of coke were weighed. A carter would lead his horse so that only the cart full of sacks of coke was on the scales. Inside the office the clerk adjusted the large beam and noted the tonnage. In the grounds, which were partly grassed, stood the enormous gas-holders. Occasionally Uncle Jim took us into the works to see the flaming coal which produced the coal gas and left the coke at the end of the process. Sometimes we were allowed to go into Uncle Jim's office, which was a kind of laboratory with bottles containing the various samples of the chemicals extracted from the coal.

One spring day in the 1920s Dad came across some Polish geese in the market at Hull, newly arrived by ship. After consulting his brother Jim they decided to buy four of them and raise them at the Gasworks. There was enough grass there to fatten them up ready for Christmas. One would be for us, one for Uncle Jim, one for their sister Margaret, a parson's wife in Glasgow, and one for Norry Abbott, the foreman at the Gasworks, who would tend the geese until the end of the year. All went according to plan and the geese were enjoyed by all. The dead goose for Aunt Margaret was sent off by rail to Glasgow with a label tied around its neck, as was the custom in those days. Nobody doubted that it would arrive safely.

At the far western side where the Westwood ends and the Walkington road begins there was a large underground reservoir. Uncle Jim took us there to look at the Artesian wells which brought fresh clean water to the surface, where it was stored in this reservoir bigger than the municipal swimming bath. Memorable also were the days when we were allowed to accompany one of the local carters on his journey delivering parcels and boxes which had arrived by rail. The carter was pleased to have us beside him as the horse slowly ambled on its way round the town. Geoff and I would leap off the seat and deliver the small parcels, leaving the carter to carry the big heavy boxes.

Geoff's brother Wid bought a dog, Chum by name. He was a frisky mongrel terrier who had much sagacity. On cricket days in the summer he would be outside the house after the midday meal waiting for Geoff to don his white flannels, mount his bike and pedal to school. At school he was well behaved and never barked. He seemed happy to watch the games without joining in. In the football season, he raced up and down the touch lines, being careful never to invade the pitch. Chum never missed a trick. When Uncle Jim and Auntie Florrie came up to Norwood to see us one evening they brought Chum with them. He was quiet and seemed to be listening to all the conversation. Suddenly Uncle Jim said to my brother David: 'Play something on the piano, David.' In those days electric lighting had not reached us in Beverley. Borrowing Uncle Jim's matches, David went into the next room, lit the gas and started playing, having placed the box of matches on the end of the piano. Suddenly he saw the door push open. In came Chum, took the matches in his teeth and returned them to Uncle Jim.

SPORTS AT B.G.S.

Cricket, football, cross-country runs, P.T.: at the Grammar School these were the activities designed to ensure that our minds had healthy bodies in which to work. Of these four, cricket for me was the one I enjoyed most. I enjoyed bowling but at batting I seldom scored more than a duck. I never came anywhere near being selected for the first eleven. When you see present-day professional cricketers wearing helmets, face guards, leg-pads, gloves and protective boxes for the nether regions, it is amazing to me that we never suffered injury or death; after all the balls were just as hard in our day. There was one accident I remember. Greenwood minor, in my form, attempting to catch a ball coming straight at him from above, received it in the middle of his forehead. He was not unconscious but a large bump appeared between his black and blue eyes.

Football I enjoyed on a bright rain-free day; but my memory is of lashing rain and muddy fields. 'Fadder' Howarth, in my form, was, like George Best, born with football in his blood. He had perfected the skill of complete control of the ball, coupled with remarkable feats of dribbling. He was a great goal scorer too, which was useful when our team was playing another school. He never, to my knowledge, became a professional footballer, but I do remember seeing his name in newspapers as a referee.

One tragedy on the football field saddened the whole school. Hoggard, a sixth-form boy in the same year as my brother David, died after injury at football when playing against a school team from Hull. We were never told what happened, but rumour spread that he had been accidentally kicked in the testicles. But, whatever the injury, he died in agony after some hours of suffering. We heard that Mr Burden had been at the hospital when he died. His coffin was carried to the grave by six of his fellow prefects, including my brother. David said that he nearly cried out in pain as the coffin dug into his shoulder. It was a sad day for the whole school, for Hoggard was a popular prefect.

My cousin Geoff and I both hated the cross-country runs on one afternoon each week and both of us regularly came home with the last half dozen. The course of the run was up Sloe Lane and on to the Westwood. At a small clump of trees known as the Triangular Bushes we turned towards the Black Mill, running over the rough grass. The prescribed course circled round the mill and then in a straight line across the grass, back to school. The distance was about two miles. Geoff and I and several others who were no good at running often attempted to crawl through the long grass, cutting out the mill. This wasn't always possible, for one of the masters supervising the run usually stationed himself and his bike at the Triangular Bushes, where he had a good view of the shirkers.

Without a gymnasium, there were no good facilities for P.T. We had no climbing ropes, 'horses' to jump over, and all the apparatus available at wealthier schools.

The annual sports day in the summer term was a welcome event, even for sluggards like me who preferred to join the spectators rather than compete. In the 1920s we had some remarkable athletes. Paddy Burden, with his great interest in the League of Nations, had welcomed several German boys to the school as boarders. One of them, a boy named Wiening, was a remarkable sprinter who smashed all existing school records. In the hundred-yards sprint, he breasted the tape several paces ahead of any others.

But of all the boys, Chris Wormald was the one whom we all cheered. He was a brilliant runner who broke all the records for the half-mile and one-mile races. Not only that; he was good at all the events including the long jump, the javelin, the high jump and many others. It was not surprising that two years running he was the Victor Ludorum. His style of running looked so effortless; with hands open and fully extended, he appeared to slice the air, his arms and legs moving with a steady rhythm. I have often wondered whether in the Grammar School archives there are any records of the times Chris Wormald achieved. After leaving school Chris worked in the offices of the East Riding County Council, playing cricket in the summer for a staff team. During the Second World War he served in the forces, but I heard that he died soon after the war of a disease he had caught in the Middle East.

AN ECLIPSE OF THE SUN

Flemmy Rogers, our history master, taught us geography as well as history which was his main subject; occasionally he would talk about astronomy and show us a map of the constellations. We were soon able to find the Great Bear, the Pole Star, Cassiopeia, Vega, Capella and Orion with his belt and sword.

One summer day in 1927 he told us that there was to be an eclipse of the sun soon after dawn on Wednesday, 29th June. 'The best place to see it will be from the top of one of the towers of Beverley Minster,' he told us. 'I've got permission for you (for he was our form-master that year) to climb the tower. So I'll meet you all at the Minster at 4.30 a.m. if you wish to go.' Every boy shot up his hand and vowed to be there. 'Don't forget to bring a piece of smoked glass,' he reminded us. 'Find an old piece of glass and hold it over a candle until it goes really black.'

How I managed to get up from my bed at 4 a.m. remains a wonder.

Beverley Minster.

Dad, Mother, David, Jean and eight-year-old Betty were up already, for they were going to walk to the Westwood, where, from the higher ground, they would have a clear view over the town towards the East. Later *The Beverley Guardian* reported that a number of Beverley families had journeyed from Beverley by train or motor to the zone of totality at Giggleswick in the West Riding of Yorkshire, where, in the school grounds, the Astronomer-Royal and his staff had encamped: *To those who stayed at home*, wrote *The Guardian* reporter, *the Westwood was the vantage ground, where hundreds assembled in the early hours to await the phenomenon, of which they had a very good view.* Cycling down to the Minster through the almost deserted town I found some of my classmates already awaiting Flemmy's arrival.

To climb the spiral stone stairway to the top of the tower you needed good lungs and a stout heart, for there must have been more than 200 steps. But we were all about thirteen years old and thought nothing of it. As we burst through the door on to the flat roof we found that the sun was already well above the horizon. There was a nip in the air although it was June. Waiting for the beginning of the eclipse, we chatted among ourselves and with Flemmy, who brought out his pipe and puffed away contentedly. Not permitted to smoke in school, he always reached for his pipe as soon as he left the school premises.

At first a few clouds passed over and we were all hoping that they would go away. Then, as the hour approached, the sky was clear. At about ten past five, through our smoked glass we saw the small segment of the moon's shadow taking a bite out of the sun. Gradually as the shadow spread across the sun our chattering ceased. A dream-like silence enveloped us as we gazed and gazed at the steady progress of the shadow. At last, for a few seconds, the sun almost disappeared. Over the red roofs of Beverley the world darkened and all the birds stopped singing. It became cold enough to make us shiver.

As it gradually became lighter and the world began to come alive, the birds repeated their morning chorus; we all burst into a hubbub of chattering. 'Boys,' said Flemmy Rogers, 'you've just seen the first total eclipse of the sun in this country for 200 years. The next one will be in the year 1999. Some of you may be alive to see that one, but I'll be long gone to kingdom come.' He lit up his pipe again. Then it was back home for breakfast and on to school again on a bright sunny June morning, so different from the eerie world we had seen briefly from the top of Beverley Minster.

More than seventy years later I was sitting in the King's Head in the Market Place at Beverley with Harry Tattersall, a former class-mate. Over a beer we were talking about the old days at the Grammar School. 'Do you remember when Flemmy Rogers took the whole class up one of the towers of the Minster to see the 1927 eclipse?' I said.

Harry shook his head. 'It wasn't all the class,' he replied. 'I wasn't there. My mother didn't wake me up in time.'

Roger of Wendover, the thirteenth-century chronicler, described an eclipse of the sun which took place nearly seven hundred years earlier, on the 14th of May, 1230:

> ... and it became so dark that the labourers, who had commenced their morning's work, were obliged to leave it, and returned home again to their beds to sleep, but in about an hour's time, to the astonishment of many, the sun regained its usual brightness.

Beverley Grammar School has always been closely associated with the Minster since the middle ages. I like to think that some of the boys on that May morning in the year 1230 had permission to climb to the top of Beverley Minster to see their eclipse. One thing is certain: their schoolmaster would not have been smoking!

A FARM ON THE MOORS

It was in 1926 that Dad and Mother decided that, for a change from the usual seaside holiday, we would all stay at a farm. Since the Great War we had mostly spent our fortnight in September at Bridlington, Filey or at the ancient town of Whitby. Somebody had told Mother and Dad about a farm on the North Yorkshire moors which took visitors in the summer. They did not advertise, depending on recommendations from those who had stayed with them.

With no public transport and no car, the problem was how to get there. Dad decided to hire a car big enough for six people and luggage. The driver gave him an estimate of the cost of taking us there and bringing us back in a fortnight. The farm was in the parish of Lockton, near the market town of Pickering about forty miles from Beverley.

From Lockton only rough tracks led to the farm. The driver rolled and bumped along these, one of us from time to time having to get out to open field gates. At last we came to Low Pastures Farm, standing alone on the moors. 'I don't know what you're all going to do with yourselves here for a fortnight,' said the driver to Dad, who was paying for the journey with what seemed to me a large number of pound notes. 'See you in a fortnight then,' said the man as he drove off.

It was all exciting for us children. Mr and Mrs Thompson, their two sturdy daughters and nineteen-year-old son Alf welcomed us heartily, showing us the bedrooms, the room where we should eat and the

Dad, Betty, Jean, Jimmy, Mother on the Yorkshire Moors, 1925.

Jimmy and a friend, 1925.

David, Betty, Jean, a friend, Jimmy at the farm, 1925.

enormous square kitchen with its peat fire. Their large farmhouse, solidly built to withstand the buffets of the strong winter winds from the moors, was primitive compared with our house in Beverley. It had no electricity or gas lighting, but we quickly became used to the daily ritual of the lighting of the oil lamps. There were no water closets, only an earth-closet in the garden, fortunately with a clump of mint growing nearby with which to make a nosegay. Mr Thompson often sat by the fire in the evening when work was finished, reading an old newspaper by the light of a candle held in one hand. No newspapers reached the farm except those bought in Pickering and there was no wireless – not even a crystal set.

On the second day we began to explore the surrounding country. About half a mile down a steep track to the valley below lived Mr and Mrs Thompson's elder son, occupying Low Staindale Farm with his wife and five-year-old Elsie. Close to their farm ran the beck into which poured fresh clean icy-cold water from the moors.

We enjoyed every minute of our farm holiday. It was the last holiday we would all have together, for David was seventeen and would soon be working in a bank. So many experiences came our way that they remain clearly in memory forever. I learned how the cream separator worked, how to take it to pieces for cleaning and how to put it together again. All of us had a go at milking the cows, with varying success. Most of us could produce a sound of milk hitting the pail, but when Dad tried there was no sound at all. Jean remembers gathering button mushrooms on the moors and picking wild brambles (blackberries) for rich pies with cream. All of us children had good appetites and we enjoyed the home-made Yorkshire curd cheesecakes.

Alf shot a fox which was prowling around the chicken-house one evening; he also killed a viper which lay in a metal bucket still writhing after death. One day Mr Thompson said that Dad could take the horse for a ride across the moors to look for a suitable place to take a couple of beehives the following year. Mother was alarmed. 'What if you get lost?,' she said. 'Don't you worry, Mrs Thirsk,' Mr Thompson replied, 'the old horse knows its own way home.' It was the first ride Dad had enjoyed since his army days. Mr Thompson suggested that he should enquire at a farm several miles away across the moors. There he found a farmer who would take his bees. 'I should put 'em up on that there bank, Maister – there's hacres and hacres of heather for them.' It was dark when Dad came back and Mother was beginning to worry.

The meals were sumptuous. Mrs Thompson's two daughters were splendid cooks, providing good Yorkshire fare. Rabbits and hares, shot by Alf or his father, soon appeared on the table as rabbit pie or jugged hare. Breakfasts were enormous and I remember with delight the sight of a large frying pan some 18 inches in diameter, hanging from an iron hook in the chimney, with a dozen fresh eggs gently frying over the peat fire. One evening, Polly, the younger daughter, apologised for the small amount of cheese for our snack after supper. It was in fact a large wedge of Wensleydale. 'We have to go to Pickering tomorrow for supplies,' she explained.

I was invited by Mr Thompson to go with him the next day to Pickering to buy food and supplies for the farm. It was a whole day trip. First, the horse and cart were made ready. I was allowed to take the reins. At Pickering we called at many different shops, with me helping to load supplies on to the open cart. Not only cheese was on the shopping list. Bacon, flour, salt, meat, tea and vinegar – all those things and many more which could not be produced on the farm. He also bought filters for the milk separator, twine, cattle cake and cartridges for his shotgun.

At the end of the fortnight we were all sad to go. The warmth of our welcome, the sunshine, the little beck in the valley – a feast of memories forever. Robert Louis Stevenson's poem *Farewell to the Farm* echoed our memories except that we left the farm in a hired car.

FAREWELL TO THE FARM

The coach is at the door at last;
The eager children, mounting fast
And kissing hands, in chorus sing:
Good-bye, good-bye to everything!

To house and garden, field and lawn,
The meadow-gates we swang upon,
To pump and stable, tree and swing,
Good-bye, good-bye to everything!

And fare you well for evermore,
O ladder at the hayloft door,
O hayloft, where the cobwebs cling,
Good-bye, good-bye, to everything!

Crack goes the whip, and off we go;
The trees and houses smaller grow;
Last, round the woody turn we swing.
Good-bye, good-bye, to everything!

ON BEVERLEY WESTWOOD

Mention Beverley Westwood to any old Beverlonians exiled from the town and you will see their faces light up. 'What wouldn't I give for a walk on the Westwood?' each one of them would say. Note *on* the Westwood and not *in*. For the Westwood is no longer a wood. Probably entirely covered with trees in prehistoric times and gradually shorn in the Middle Ages and later, it is now a spacious common of some 500 acres, about a mile across and the same from east to west. A few trees remain, mostly in the old limestone quarries now grassed over; at the far western boundary, near the race-course, are Burton Bushes, a remnant of the old forest.

As you enter the Westwood from the direction of York, descending from the East Riding wolds, a route travelled on horseback by Celia Fiennes and later by Daniel Defoe, when they each visited Beverley, the road drops into the town. As you descend the slope you can see the Black Mill across the grassland and wooded areas, with the towers of St Mary's and Beverley Minster in the distance.

Each of us in the family and everybody who lives or has lived in Beverley has his or her special memories of the Westwood. For some the magic of it covered with snow is their happiest memory. 'Ally ally aster snow snow faster!' we would chant as the first snowflakes fell. Out would come the old toboggan from the garden shed, its runners rusty again, but soon shining bright after the application of emery paper and elbow-grease. Dad made our toboggan; it was built like an army tank, with heavy timber sides and wooden slatted seats painted scarlet and was big enough for four adults or half a dozen children. Not so swift as some of the lighter models, it nevertheless had a majestic appearance as it gathered speed on Hill 60. In those days a small circular pond stood at the bottom of that hill, often frozen over in winter but in summer an oasis for roaming cows.

In the years just after the Great War we often went for picnics on the Westwood as we had done during the war when Dad was away. Other families took picnics, but there was plenty of room and it was always possible to find a shady place near the trees where we felt that we had the place to ourselves.

Although I enjoyed my friendship with a small group of class-mates who used to gather together after school for adventures before going home, there were times when I wished to be alone, to wander on the Westwood on foot or on bike.

Through frequent reading of my favourite book *Robinson Crusoe*, I often wished that I too could be alone on a desert island and be self-sufficient, far away from the daily round of school, homework and bed. One summer morning, waking very early to find the sun just rising, I slipped out of bed, donned shirt, trousers and gym-shoes (trainers didn't exist) and crept quietly out of the house. Down Norwood, up Hengate, Wood Lane and Little Woodlands I sped through the deserted streets; within ten minutes I was on the Westwood enjoying the sunshine and knowing that it was unlikely that anybody from the sleeping town was there. It must have been in late May or early June, for the pink hawthorn trees were all in bloom. In Newbegin Pits, the first group of trees you come to, the birds were singing and I heard the chimes of Beverley Minster and of St Mary's tolling 6 o'clock. Intoxicated with this preview of paradise, I suddenly took off all my clothes and like Adam was monarch of all I surveyed. To gain a better view of my possessions, I climbed a tree and sat on a branch, shivering slightly in the breeze and thinking of Tarzan in Africa in the steaming jungle.

The Hull poet Andrew Marvell would have recognised my bliss:

Two Paradises 'twere in one
To live in Paradise alone.

I nearly fell out of the tree when a man's loud voice from about fifty yards away roused me from my dreams. 'Have you seen a black and white cow?' he called to me. It was the cowman rounding up his herd which had been wandering all over the Westwood during the night. 'No,' I shouted back from the top of the tree, wondering whether he had seen that I had no clothes on. Back home again, nobody seemed to have missed me. I had a good appetite for breakfast; then it was off to school as usual on my bike.

ARMISTICE DAY

The Great War ended at 1100 hours on the 11th of November, 1918, or, as we used to say, 'at the eleventh hour of the eleventh day of the eleventh month.' That was when all hostilities ceased between Germany and the Allies, after the signing of an armistice at 0500 hours the same day, in a railway carriage in the Forest of Compiègne in Northern France.

Armistice Day, or Remembrance Day, as it was later called, has been celebrated ever since. In the 1920s and 1930s a two minutes silence was observed by almost everybody at exactly 11 a.m. on the 11th of November every year. At Beverley Grammar School, in the 1920s, the Headmaster, Paddy Burden, gathered the whole school together, with all the masters, in the double class-room which was used for morning assembly. We knew exactly the time of the two-minute silence which was signalled by the loud report of a rocket fired

Memorial recording the Beverley Grammar School boys who died in World War II (Beverley Minster).

in the centre of the town, the same rocket which summoned the part-time firemen to duty.

When the silence ended, a senior prefect went to the back of the room to read aloud from a memorial tablet on the wall the names of the former Grammar School boys who had died during the war. The ceremony ended with the singing of the National Anthem. The solemnity of the occasion impressed us all deeply. Many of the boys had lost fathers, brothers, uncles and cousins, or were living with those who had survived but who were wounded.

In the town, the Mayor and Corporation observed the ceremony, accompanied by soldiers of the East Yorkshire Regiment, based at Beverley barracks. They would end the silence with buglers sounding the Last Post. At school we had a Cadet Corps who wore their uniforms on the day. I do not remember a bugle, which would have been too loud in the confined space of our makeshift assembly hall.

It was, I remember, in 1924, when I was ten years old, that I was off school for almost the whole autumn term, afflicted by colitis. On Remembrance Day that year Dad was at work and David and Jean were at school. Mother and I and Betty, who was too young for school, were at home. I had a bright idea: in the garden shed were several mementos which Dad had brought back home from France. There was his old steel helmet, his spurs, a gas-mask and a British bayonet. I brought the bayonet into the house and stood to attention in the front room. Then, as the rocket signalled the beginning of the two minute silence, I drew the bayonet from its guard, holding it upright in my hand. Who knows what goes on in the head of a ten-year old? Perhaps I thought I was defying the forces of evil; or perhaps I was jealous of Dad because he had taken part in the defeat of Germany and I had not. Or perhaps, because I was ill, I wished to show that I could not be defeated.

At the beginning of the Great War, in 1914, H. G. Wells published a pamphlet with the title: *The War That Will End War*. He was too optimistic, for, only a little more than twenty years after the peace treaty was signed at Versailles, World War II began. After the war, in 1920, H. G. Wells corrected his mistake, fearing that before a future world state came, with no more wars, there might be further struggles and conflicts leading to the 'misery and slaughter of generations.' How right he was! He firmly believed that the future of mankind was dependent on 'a race between education and catastrophe.' Marshal Foch, Commander of the Allied forces, was overheard saying at the Peace Conference in 1919: *'Ce n'est pas un traité de paix, c'est un armistice de vingt ans.'* (It isn't a peace treaty – it's a twenty-year armistice.)

On a wall inside Beverley Minster there are two memorial tablets bearing the names of the Grammar School boys who died or were killed in the Second World War. Among them are the names of four of my class-mates and of my brother David. He lies in a grave in Italy, near Milan, with all the crew of a Lancaster bomber.

Atque in perpetuum, frater, ave atque vale!'
(And forever, brother, hail and farewell!)

These are the closing words of a poem by Catullus, written after visiting his brother's grave.

FRENCH LESSONS

Now, fie upon my false French!

Henry V

For the first two years in Form I at Beverley Grammar School we had no French lessons. But from my brother David, more than five years older, I heard many stories about the French master, Mr H. M. Ross, who was the senior teacher in the school and Deputy Headmaster. He had taught at the school since 1906 and was affectionately known by everybody as 'Pa' Ross. He was a tall, broad, imposing man of whom most of the boys were in awe. His fierce aspect was made even more fearsome by a monocle in his right eye, which at appropriate moments he would release, leaving it dangling at the end of a cord around his neck. Pa Ross retired in 1924 just before my class started learning French.

At that time the French textbook in use was *Heath's Practical French Grammar*. Each chapter began with rules of grammar, followed by exercises. 'You can't do the exercises,' Pa Ross would roar at the thirty boys in the class, followed, in a gentle voice, almost a whisper by: 'unless you read the rules.' David imitated Pa Ross's voice and told me that one of his trick questions, which he trotted out every term, was to point to a gullible boy. 'Conjugate *mouchoir*,' he would say. The poor youth, knowing his verb-endings, would commence: *'Je mouche, tu mouches, il mouche, nous mouchons . . .'* By the time he reached *'mouchons,'* Pa Ross would interrupt him with a roar. 'Nonsense, boy! *Le mouchoir* is the handkerchief.' The class never forgot the word. Occasionally, in Form I, when our woman teacher, Mrs Watson, was absent, Pa Ross would supervise us. We found him a gentle, kind man, not the roaring ogre we heard about from the older boys.

He was succeeded by Isaac Simpson, a first-class honours graduate in French and German from Leeds University. 'Ikey,' as he was soon named, was not a roaring man; by contrast he never raised his voice in anger. He endeared himself to most of the boys by his sarcastic comments on behaviour, which always earned a laugh. I remember that one day my class-mate, Ken Annakin, who later became a film director, yawned noisily without covering his mouth. 'Léonard,' said Ikey, (for he had given us all French forenames – mine was Sébastien), 'in polite circles it is usual to cover one's mouth when yawning. If your hand is not large enough, use your *Heath's* grammar and if that does not suffice, raise your desk lid.'

Ikey's pronunciation of French was magnificent; at least we thought so, although none of us had ever heard a real Frenchman speak. It was a pleasure to hear him reading a passage during a dictation lesson. At the end of every term Ikey would forget the exercises, the compositions and the dictations; instead, on the last lesson, he would read short stories, translating them as he spoke. In this way he introduced us to Guy de Maupassant, Anatole France and others. One of the poems which Ikey made us learn by heart told the story of *Le grand Lustucru,* a terrifying monster who passed down the streets at night dragging his chains on the cobbles. He was seeking to devour the little boys and girls who would not go to sleep. I remember how Ikey rolled the 'r' sound as he pronounced *Lustucru.* This lullaby, sung by French mothers, would have been more likely to give the children nightmares than put them to sleep.

> *C'est le grand Lustucru qui passe.*
> *C'est le grand Lustucru qui mangera*
> *Tous les petits gars qui ne dorment guère*
> *Tous les petits gars qui ne dorment pas!*

We were all sorry when Ikey left us to go to a better paid job at a college in Newcastle; sorry also that his successor, Mr Davies, spoke French with a distinct Welsh accent. We all began to lose interest in French. Paddy Burden, the Headmaster, must have been aware that things were not going too well with our French lessons. Because we were nearing the time of the School Certificate examination, usually taken at 16 years of age, he decided to give us a weekly lesson himself. For a whole term he went through every sentence of Guy de Maupassant's story *Boule de suif.* His accent was nowhere near that of Ikey, but, as with all subjects, he was a great teacher.

Memories of *Heath's Practical French Grammar* come back to me. In the second part of the book, after the exercises based on the rules, there were many short pieces of English prose, which we had to translate into French. Some of them were old fables and others short stories some fifty or sixty words long. These I loved to read, even though it was unlikely that we would translate them all. One of them amused me and my friends. It was about Bernardin de Saint-Pierre, the French writer famous for his moving love story: *Paul et Virginie* (1788). Leaving Moscow after a visit to Russia, he was surrounded by barking dogs. Stooping down to pick up a stone, he found that it was frozen in the earth. *'Never again,'* said he, *'will I come to such a country, where the dogs are so fierce and the stones are fast in the ground.'* Another story told of a young man, walking-stick in hand, setting out one morning on a journey into the country. After some time the landscape became familiar as if he had known it many years before. But where and when? This passage still haunts me. No author was given but I am hoping that some day I will find it in a book.

One of these stories Ikey Simpson asked us to translate into French. When he had corrected our efforts he made us learn it by heart. After all these years I can still recall it. The story was about a baker in a village in France who bought his butter from a local farmer. Thinking he was being cheated, he accused the farmer of supplying underweight butter. The case came to court and the judge asked the farmer to bring his scales and weights into the court: *'Je n'en ai pas,' répondit le fermier. 'Alors, comment pesez-vous votre beurre,' dit le juge de paix. 'Ah, c'est très simple,' dit le fermier. 'J'achète des pains de deux kilos chez le boulanger chaque semaine, et je m'en sers pour peser les deux kilos de beurre que je lui envoie chaque samedi.'* The English title of this story, *The Biter Bit*, we translated as *'Le trompeur trompé'*.

After the School Certificate French paper there was an oral examination. This was conducted by an unknown French teacher from another school. We were all apprehensive because little attention had been devoted to easy conversation. Also our French pronunciation had probably been corrupted by Mr Davies's Welsh accent. Those who survived the ordeal and passed the examination were pleasantly surprised.

AMO AMAS I LOVE A LASS

Latin is a language
As dead as dead can be.
It killed the ancient Romans
And now it's killing me!
      Anon.

We should all have been good Latin scholars at Beverley Grammar School for two reasons. Firstly, our school motto was understood by every boy. We soon learned that the words *Adolescentiam alunt, senectutem oblectant* referred to literature and books, which 'nourish youth and are the solace of old age.' The Latin words appeared, stamped in gold, on the front cover of the book, presented to you if you were clever enough to receive a school prize. Secondly, a notable classical scholar came to Beverley Grammar School at the age of eleven, setting us a good example.

John Conington (1825-1869) only stayed at Beverley a couple of years before moving on to Rugby School and Magdalen College, Oxford. Later he was appointed to a newly-founded Chair of Latin language and literature at the University of Oxford at the age of twenty-nine, remaining a professor until his early death in 1869, at the age of forty-four. During this time he translated in verse some Horace, Virgil's *Aeneid*, and many other classical works. John Conington is said to have had an extraordinary memory and once, at the age of eight, he recited to his father a thousand lines of Virgil. Most of us found it difficult to remember even twenty. He is remembered by the naming of one of the school 'houses' Conington, of which my brother David and I were members.

Alas, after such an example of scholarship, none of my classmates achieved any proficiency in Latin. This dead language never came to life in the classes of three successive teachers. The first was Mr Milligan, a Scotsman from Glasgow University, whose strong native accent had invaded his Latin pronunciation. He had been in the army during the Great War. He was a tough, wiry man and it was said that he could turn a complete somersault in the air; but none of us had witnessed this feat. He moved on and was followed by Mr Ken Bidmead ('Biddy'), a graduate of Bristol University. Biddy had no strong accent that I remember. It was, I believe, his first post after graduation. He was young in appearance and looked no older than some of the boys in the 6th Form. I remember him demonstrating the steps of the Charleston, one of the popular dances of the 1920s.

Perhaps of my three Latin teachers the next and last was the one who tried to blow on the embers of the dead language harder than his predecessors. P. J. Morgan was a Welshman, well liked by most boys. He had played football for Wales in a junior team and was still physically fitter than any master in the school. Because of this he was put in charge of most of the P.T. classes, which he conducted with relish, delighting in demonstrations of his own agility and suppleness. When occasionally some of the masters joined senior games of football, Mr Morgan showed us that he had not forgotten the skills he had learned as a junior champion.

I can still hear his rhyming advice on a point of Latin grammar:

> *With ask, advise, command and strive*
> *By* ut *translate the infinitive*

This couplet was spoken in his forthright Welsh voice, tempting one to add 'Look you!' at the end.

The pronunciation of Latin caused hilarity at times, particularly the pronunciation of words beginning with the letter V. My Dad, who had been taught Latin and Greek at a village school in Fife, laughed at our pronunciation of V as a W. He was sure that Julius Caesar said *Veni, vidi, vici* (I came, I saw, I conquered), not *Weni, widi, wici,* which was the way we were taught to say it. Dad was a great believer in the importance of a grounding in Latin. When we stumbled over the meaning of a word at home he would exclaim: 'Where's your Latin? What do I pay all these school fees for?' And for all the years of Latin studies what did we learn? That anybody could converse with another in Latin, or read and understand Latin with ease seemed unbelievable; most of us left school knowing a few Latin tags and very little else.

The teaching of Latin was uninspiring and it would surely have been better if it had concentrated on learning more about life in ancient Greece and Italy; and how much more useful it would have been to study the roots of English, by learning the key words in Latin and Greek that make up such a large part of the English language.

ENGLISH LITERATURE

Willie Burrow, our English teacher for most of my days at Beverley Grammar School, was an honours graduate of the University of London. Had fate turned him in the direction of the stage he would have become a notable actor; for he had the actor's voice and, although not robust physically, commanded attention by his theatrical gestures. Children love schoolmasters who are good actors; they also love teachers who do not lose their tempers. Willie, like Ikey Simpson, the French master, reproved boys with wit and sarcasm, which was always appreciated by the rest of the class. Seeing my friend Mark Pottage picking his nose one day, Mr Burrow interrupted his discourse with these words: 'I'm surprised to see that a boy who rejoices in the name of James Markham Pottage should behave in this manner. People in the best circles of society do not endeavour to see how far up their noses they can push their fingers.'

Willie loved literature and wished us to enjoy the authors we read. Usually at the end of term he would read to us a short story by Edgar Allan Poe in a voice that held us spellbound. His reading of Poe's *The Pit and the Pendulum* was unforgettable, as was a frightening chapter from Charles Reade's novel, *The Cloister and the Hearth.* Coleridge was one of his favourite writers and his recital of *The Ancient Mariner* was wonderful to hear:

All in a hot and copper sky
The bloody sun at noon
Right high above the mast did seem
No bigger than the moon.

The ice was here, the ice was there,
The ice was all around;
It crack'd and groan'd and roared and howl'd
Like noises in a swound.

I can still hear Willie's voice as he recited these two verses.

Willie left Beverley Grammar School in 1928, moving to a teacher training college near Birmingham. He never married and in retirement at Stratford-upon-Avon lived with an unmarried sister. Shakespeare was one of the great loves of his life; in later years he told me that he read a passage from the plays every day, gradually re-reading them all. He had enjoyed his teaching at Beverley and he never forgot the happy days there. Death came swiftly for Willie, at the age of about seventy; for several years he had been having attacks of angina. The end came at home when he collapsed after a car drive from Yorkshire to Stratford-upon-Avon.

Our next English teacher after Willie Burrow was a young man newly graduated from the University of Oxford. Many years later I learned that he had been interviewed by our Headmaster on Manchester railway station. Norman Dawson, by contrast with Willie, was tall, broad-shouldered, with auburn hair. There was something of the Viking about him in appearance, although instead of being warlike he had an Olympian calm. Smoking was forbidden in school except in the staff-room, but outside he was seldom seen without a pipe in his mouth.

His commentaries on the set books we had to study showed how widely he had read. He inspired some of us to read with enjoyment. Some poems by Matthew Arnold were on the syllabus, and Mr Dawson, who never had a nickname, gave us, when we read *The Scholar Gypsy,* his own memories of the Oxfordshire countryside, which he obviously knew well. In his company we traced the wanderings of the mysterious Scholar Gypsy on the Cumnor hills, past the Fyfield elm and crossing *the stripling Thames at Bab-lock-hithe.*

He was not a man who was roused to anger by inattention. One day when a boy was twanging a 12-inch ruler in class, Mr Dawson, without interrupting what he was saying, walked to the boy's desk, took the ruler, broke it into pieces and dropped it in the wastepaper basket as he returned to the front of the class. 'But Sir, that was an expensive ruler,' exclaimed the boy. No reply came and the class continued. Mr Dawson left the school after two years, in 1930, having found a post at a school in the Midlands. I left Beverley Grammar School at the same time and I have no knowledge of the succeeding English teachers.

In the 1930s, the old *Manchester Guardian,* now *The Guardian,* often printed short stories, one column in length, by non-professional writers. I saw one of these stories signed ND, about a young teacher trying to interest a class of boys in the glories of English literature. It was a pessimistic story, with the young teacher imagining a long bleak future teaching unresponsive boys. I was sure it was by Mr Dawson. I should have written to him care of the *Manchester Guardian.* But I didn't. However, nearly 60 years later, I was given his name and address in Cumbria. When I wrote to him, I reminded him of his pessimistic story in the *Manchester Guardian* and assured him that some of his old students had relished his classes, which had led them on to explore many byways in English literature. Here is my letter and his reply:

The Kilns
Lewis Close
OXFORD
OX3 8JD
4 December 1983

Dear Mr Dawson

Some time ago a friend came to see my wife and me in Oxford on the occasion of a St Edmund Hall annual reunion. 'If you see any older members of the college,' I said, 'ask them if they remember N. Dawson.' Afterwards he told me that one old member did remember you. He also found for me your name and address in a list of old members of 'Teddy Hall.'

So I am writing a thank-you letter which really I should have written about fifty years ago. I remember reading in the 1930s a short story on the back page of the old *Manchester Guardian,* by ND. The theme was the despair of an English teacher faced with a class of teenagers. Their blank reception of his talk of the glories of literature made him wonder whether such a life was worth living. A very melancholy tale! If it is any comfort to you now there were several of us who enjoyed your classes at Beverley Grammar School and who still speak of you with great affection. One of them, a lifelong friend, is Oliver – or Noll as he is still known. He played Snug the Joiner in your production of *A Midsummer Night's Dream.* But names from those antediluvian days must mean nothing to you now among all the thousands of later pupils you have known. I'm sure however that you will remember the name Ibbotson, who left school to run his father's tobacconist shop in Toll Gavel. He is still in the land of the living, but no longer handing out tins of Capstan full-strength, which I trust you have now given up. Partly because he was our friend and partly because of your example, we all became pipe-smokers. His shop was a regular meeting place for a group of us and there he mixed up various tobaccos – usually with a dash of Latakia.

We were very lucky at Beverley Grammar School to have had two such inspiring teachers of English as you and your predecessor Mr Burrow. I remember very clearly your talk about Oxford and the Oxford countryside when we were studying Arnold's *The Scholar Gypsy*. Most of us had never been outside the East Riding of Yorkshire and you brought glimpses of the outer world and gave some of us an appetite for the treasures of English literature, still not satisfied.

After a lifetime in librarianship, mainly working in public libraries, I retired about nine years ago. My wife was a Reader in Economic History here in Oxford and has just retired this summer. We live in the house where C. S. Lewis lived for about thirty years – on the lower slopes of Shotover Hill. Did you ever attend his lectures in the 1920s? Many American disciples come to look at the house in the summer time and they seem to be more interested in his religious writings than are the English.

We are trying to sell the house at present because we intend to move to a village near Tonbridge. Do please let me know if you ever come to Oxford. It would be a great delight to see you again. With best wishes and thanks for your wise words all those years ago. And best wishes also for Christmas and 1984.

Yours sincerely

Jim Thirsk

Auburn
Kentsford Road
Kents Bank Cumbria
LA11 7BB
11th December,1983

Dear Jim Thirsk

It would be hard to persuade you how much I appreciated your letter without sounding very fulsome. It recalled my teaching days so vividly – and they are a long way back.

You were wrong about one thing however. I remember everything at Beverley clearly. And I can see the faces of Ibbotson and Oliver with ease. I wonder how they have changed over the years. Strangely enough I never returned to Beverley until a couple of years ago, when a letter out of the blue from Percy Morgan persuaded me to go back for an Old Boys' dinner. I did renew a few acquaintances if not so many as I had hoped, but the experience made me wonder if I could have recognised any of them but for the occasion and the setting.

Beverley was most important to me. I had never intended to be a schoolmaster. I had ambitions for Fleet Street at that time. When they did not immediately work out I found myself about to be penniless, but was rescued by Paddy Burden literally a month before the autumn term of 1928. He interviewed me on Exchange Station, Manchester! Two years at Beverley confirmed me in a decision I never regretted – to stay in the teaching job. (That in spite of the back page article in the old *Manchester Guardian.*) So Beverley has a lot to answer for.

After Beverley I had two years at Edward VI, Nuneaton, and six years at St Albans School. I then left for my first headship at the Heversham Grammar School, Westmorland. My real teaching days ended with that change of job. I think that is why I was moved by your letter. It is a far cry to my ten years as an English teacher, and I think that they were, professionally at any rate, my happiest.

When I went to St Albans some joker in the staff-room christened me 'Nat,' and Nat I have stayed ever since, even to my wife and children and grandchildren. I often think that is why I have lost touch with many from the old days who would have kept in touch but for whom the name means nothing.

My last Headship was at the Glyn School, Epsom, from 1951-1967. The last few years were overshadowed by the death of my wife and I retired at 61 and came back to the north-west as we had always intended. I began a voluntary and virtually full-time career as Chairman of the Cumbria Trust for Nature Conservation, but after eleven years I decided I had better hand over before senility set in. I still, however, work quite steadily as Vice-President. And I find time for quite a lot of wildlife photography. (My elder daughter lives in Colorado, so I do quite a lot of travel in USA.)

Pondering on your letter, I work out somewhat to my surprise that probably the oldest boy I knew at Beverley was Lythe, and that he would now be around 73. So your amazing claim to 69 has to be accepted.

You do touch my conscience very severely about the pipe-smoking. No, I have not smoked for a quarter of a century. But who was to know then? Anyway, it was a *pipe*, and not cigarettes.

I never heard C. S. Lewis lecture. Gilbert Murray's name was the one to conjure with in my time. On the whole they were a pretty dull lot in my day. I came to have a lot of respect for Leavis later on (at the other place, of course), though I think he, and his scions could be insufferably pious at times. Not 'pious.' 'Precious' is the word I wanted. I sent him quite a number of English students on scholarships – one or two of them very gifted indeed.

Even though my younger daughter lives in Oxfordshire I never seem to travel south. She and her family come here every holiday. But if I do come south I will certainly look you up.

Your letter caused a welter of reminiscence, and I am going to use that, and not old age, as an excuse for this rather rambling reply.
All good wishes
Yours very sincerely
Nat Dawson

P.S. Your Teddy Hall card reminded me of a snap sent to me by my younger daughter only a week or two ago, showing my five grandchildren standing at the well in the quad. (The three from America were over here on a visit.) It was cleverly angled to show staircase number 1, where I had rooms fifty-nine years ago. But your card showed the mock acacia where I saw my first nuthatch. (A bit worse for wear now, I am afraid.) I wrote about it quite a lot of years ago in *The Countryman*.

For two years we corresponded occasionally and I showed the letters to three old school friends, one of whom wrote to Nat. One summer I was travelling in Cumbria. Hoping to meet him at his home near Grange-over-Sands, I telephoned. There was no reply. He told me later that he was visiting his daughter in America at the time.

In October 1986 a letter came from his daughter Ann to tell me that Nat had a stroke and fell off a ladder while gardening. He died soon after without recovering consciousness. With the letter she enclosed a colour photograph of an American red fox, taken by her father that summer on the prairies of Wyoming. On the morning of the day he died he had been working in his dark-room, producing prints of his fox, which he intended to mount on his Christmas cards that year.

THE FAMOUS EXPLORER KRISTH

In the spring of 1930, my last year at school, Mr Dawson, the English teacher, asked us all to write an essay for homework on the subject of exploration. He did not say whether he wanted fact or fiction, so I decided to invent a story, believing that the task would be easier. At that time I had been reading some of the novels of H. Rider Haggard, especially those in which that indomitable explorer Allan Quartermain took part. In my story, inspired partly by Rider Haggard, I became the great Norwegian explorer Kristh (an anagram of Thirsk, my surname). My companion was Vilreo (one of my school friends Oliver) and their faithful companion, a polar-bear named Ernskin, was another school friend, Skinner. Also in the story was Swanod (Mr Dawson himself), an Icelandic warrior.

Mr Dawson gave me full marks for the story but he was at first

49

sceptical about its originality. 'Where did you read this story, Thirsk?' he asked me. I was a little upset by his doubts. ' I wrote it out yesterday at home, Sir, out of my head,' I replied. In the end he did believe me. 'It's just the sort of piece I want for the next issue of the school magazine,' he said.

So here is the story, as it appeared in the *The Beverlonian*, in July 1930.

A FAMOUS EXPLORER

Few people living now remember Kristh, the Norwegian explorer who lived in the last century between the years 1816 and 1896. To his intimate friends he was known as 'Satan,' not because he was a wicked man, but because of his gnarled face and keen eyes, which some said resembled those of the 'evil one.' He was short and thick-set, possessing wonderful strength in the body and was well-known for his daring. At the age of twenty-two his adventurous life began. He had one human companion, who had saved his life when a boy, and who went with him on all his explorations. This youth was even shorter and much more thick-set than Kristh and also possessed great strength. His name was Siepmann Vilreo. The two were locked in a close bond of friendship, to be severed only by death. The third member of all their world-famous expeditions was a she-bear of vast bulk, of the type known as the Polar bear. They had caught her on one of their earlier expeditions in Greenland, finding her destitute – a small sprawling cub. They had at once named her Ernskin, the 'ern' being the Norse for 'white as snow' and 'skin' being taken from the English.

This bear was most ferocious, but it followed Kristh about like a shadow and many times proved its faithfulness to him. All men who spoke harshly either to Kristh or to Vilreo were in danger of their lives; but Ernskin was obedient and never fought unless at Satan's command.

To recount all their adventures would be tedious and unnecessary, since they form the subject of many books; but one exploit, the most thrilling, and, in my opinion, their highest endeavour, has never yet been fully narrated. Let me transcribe first the newspaper cutting which I have now beside me as I write:

The world-famous and intrepid explorer Kristh has recently expressed his opinion that the Continent around the South Pole, so far hardly explored, contains in the interior a tribe of peoples, perhaps different in form from us. Mr Kristh has been impressed by many traces which he saw when last there. He is shortly to make another expedition into this world of snow and ice.

Shortly after this date Kristh set out in his whaler, a specially fitted ship, designed by himself. He spent much time preparing supplies, and took only four other sailors with him, who remained with the ship on the coast. They were instructed to wait there for two months and then to sail for home. How comic they would look, those two men and a bear, setting out on foot across the ice. In their huge furs Kristh and Vilreo must have been nearly as broad as tall, for they were both short. The bear, in her natural fur, pulled a small swift sled with ease, and with her half stooping, shambling gait, no doubt cut a laughable figure.

After many days walking, and many nights huddled over a smoking stove in their bivouac, one evening, like Robinson Crusoe they found a footprint in the snow! The bear grunted, and sniffed apprehensively at the clear track. The two explorers quickly bivouacked; the bear, as usual, kept guard outside, where it never suffered from cold for obvious reasons. The next morning the two companions set out, carefully following the footprints, and bivouacked at night as before. The moonlight night was still comparatively young, when both men were awakened by a deep grunt, followed by the sound of a scuffle; then, after a muffled scream, silence once more drifted down the still banks of snow.

The sight which met our eyes, said Kristh in his memoirs, *as we stepped out of the tent, was one which we shall never forget. The vast white shape of our faithful bear was silhouetted against the deep blue, not quite black sky, peculiar to the Polar night. Her panting breath, hoary in the cold, showed up like incense in the moonlight. All around the desolate wastes of snow undulated away and the intense solitude and numbing of the senses, can only be realised by the true Polar explorer. Calling off the bear, we saw beneath, a tall man, about seven feet high and certainly of no known race. His dress and appearance were similar to that of the old Vikings. His long yellow hair streamed out below a helmet and a soft yellow beard flowed down on to his breast. There he lay, silent in the stillness. The next morning we stripped him of various curiosities; one was a collar of metal not unlike gold around his neck, which had some unknown letters inscribed on it. These afterwards we found to be the Icelandic word 'Swanod,' which was presumably his name.*

The two explorers continued into the interior and the following extract from the diary gives us a vivid account of their next experience:

One morning, we found ourselves looking from the top of a hill of ice, deep down into a valley wreathed in mist. There we saw vaguely the stone walls of a town or city and outside, a mass of people who clamoured round them.

But the two friends had pushed on at once over the limit of the time they had allowed themselves and were nearly to the end of their supplies. Reluctantly Kristh turned his steps towards home, for he would fain have explored further; but he realised that he had only ten days left in which to reach safety. Striking northwards, carrying with them as many relics from the dead man as possible, they at length reached the coast, luckily not more than one mile from the ship. The four sailors were preparing to depart, according to orders.

Such is the adventure of Kristh and his companion. Let who will explain it. The most feasible explanation I heard is that some branch of one of the northern peoples travelled from the main stock many thousands of years ago and, becoming inured to the cold, has dwelt there since. The Icelandic writing on the ring supports this theory, but possibly no one will ever know the truth. No one may find the 'snow city' again unless by chance as did Kristh and Vilreo.

Kristh lived to be an old man, exiling himself from the world, mourning the loss of his old companions, who were unfortunately both killed in a later adventure. In the year in which he died, Kristh fitted out a ship and sailed for the Antarctic. There he had himself marooned on the fringe of the snowy wastes, sending his ship home. It was understood by those aboard that he intended to proceed by forced marches inland until the end came; thus he chose to meet his death in the snowy haunts where he had experienced the most thrilling moments of his vivid life.

The End

Mr Dawson made no comment on my casting him in the role of Swanod, the Icelandic warrior.

Fifty years after I had written this story, a biography of one of the greatest English explorers of all time, Harold William Tilman (1898-1978?) was published. The author was J. R. L. Anderson and the title of the book, *High mountains and cold seas*. When I read this book, it reminded me of my famous explorer Kristh. Tilman also had this yearning to be in Antarctica in old age; both he and Kristh were eighty years old when they died.

Tilman began his career as a young soldier on the Western Front in the Great War. Surviving the war he became a daring mountaineer and explorer in Africa and Central Asia. After service again in the Army, in the Second World War, in which he was awarded a D.S.O. (in the Great War an M.C. with Bar), he gave up mountaineering in his fifties and took to the sea, joining expeditions to the Arctic and the Antarctic. He was seventy-six years old when he circumnavigated Spitzbergen in his cutter *Baroque*. At seventy-nine he joined an expedition to Smith Island in the South Shetlands, hoping to spend his eightieth birthday in Antarctica. The ship, the *En Avant,* disappeared with all hands.

AMATEUR DRAMATICS

Mr Norman Dawson, our English teacher, produced only two plays during the two years he was at the school. The first was a medieval play *The Harrowing of Hell*. Dramas of this kind, known as mystery plays, became popular in England from the 13th century up to Shakespeare's time. Similar productions were known in most European countries and it is likely that they were seen at Beverley Minster in the Middle Ages. Produced by some of the guilds, they were designed to make known to their audiences the great stories from the Bible. Sometimes comic scenes were inserted to enliven the action; in one play about Noah and the Flood, Mrs Noah refused to enter the Ark.

In *The Harrowing of Hell*, based on the legend that Jesus descended into hell to rescue those wrongly condemned, Mr Dawson played the part of Satan. A tall, powerful, well-built man, he wielded an enormous club. One of my class-mates, Keech, was chosen for the part of one of Satan's devils. It was good casting, for he was an agile, muscular boy who trained regularly in the gymnasium at Beverley

Midsummer Night's Dream, *1929.*
Ken Annakin (Peter Quince); extreme left; John Baker (Bottom); centre; Raymond Oliver (Noll) as Snug, the joiner: 2nd from right.

Barracks, where his father was a soldier in the East Yorkshire Regiment. He and the minor devils, clad in red skin-tight costumes, pranced about outside the mouth of Hell. Keech raised the biggest laughs, performing hand springs and unusual contortions, to the great delight of the audience. From the mouth of Hell, constructed by boys in the carpentry shed, Eric Cross, our chemistry master, produced smoke, flames and noxious gases.

Willie Burrow, Mr Dawson's predecessor, an English teacher who might well have been an actor had not fate intervened, amused his class with his histrionic abilities. One of his productions for the school was the short play *Waterloo*, a favourite in the 1890s, staged many times in London and the provinces by Sir Henry Irving and once at Windsor Castle by special request of Queen Victoria. Based on a short story by Conan Doyle entitled *The Straggler of the '15*, the play tells the story of a ninety-year old survivor of the battle of Waterloo. Now a cantankerous old man, Corporal Brewster, played by Willie Burrow himself, had been a young Guardsman who saved the day at Waterloo by bringing up wagon-loads of gunpowder in face of the enemy. He was given a medal by the Duke of Wellington. Old Brewster lives alone at first and is constantly criticising life in the 1880s and comparing it with the golden days of his youth. His hero was the Duke of Wellington, the victor of Waterloo. 'It wouldn't have done for the Duke', is his constant cry. It was a perfect part for Willie Burrow, who delighted us boys with his portrayal of the old veteran.

Willie Burrow played a major part in the production of the Gilbert and Sullivan comic operas. I do not remember that he directed a Shakespeare play, but another of his productions was the Gilbert Murray translation of *Oedipus Rex* by Sophocles, which must have shocked some of the parents. Oedipus, in Greek legend, unwittingly kills his father, Laius, King of Thebes, and marries his mother, Jocasta. On learning later what he has done, he blinds himself. Jocasta, his wife and mother, commits suicide. Willie, playing the part of the unhappy Oedipus, was a towering figure. I can still see him in his agony, standing at the front of the stage facing the audience, with bloody, bandaged eye-sockets and outstretched arms. A gruesome sight for Beverlonians!

Mr Dawson produced only one play by Shakespeare. *A Midsummer Night's Dream* was the set book in the year we sat for the School Certificate examination (the equivalent of the present G.C.S.E.). Most of the actors came from my form. My friend Oliver was Snug, the joiner, one of the 'rude mechanicals.' Playing the part of the lion he had only one line to remember:

> *Have you the Lions part written? Pray, if it be, give it me, for I am slow of study.*

Peter Quince, the producer of the play *Pyramus and Thisbe,* the play within the play, replies: *You may do it extempore, for it is nothing but roaring.*

Ken Annakin, who played the part of Peter Quince, the carpenter, became in later life a film director, with such films as *The Battle of the Bulge, Those Magnificent Men in their Flying Machines* and *The Swiss Family Robinson* to his credit. Outstanding among my classmates, however, was John Edward Baker, who played the part of Bottom the Weaver with great gusto. Baker, probably the noisiest boy in our class, was ideal in the part. He strutted about the stage declaring loudly that he had the ability to play not only the lion but Thisbe, Pyramus's girl-friend, as well.

Let me play the Lion too, he shouts.

But Peter Quince flatters Bottom, convincing him that Pyramus is the part he must play:

You can play no part but Pyramus, for Pyramus is a sweet-fac'd man; a proper man as one shall see in a summer's day; a most lovely gentleman-like man; therefore you must needs play Pyramus.

I took no part in this production, being content to sell programmes at the entrance. But I enjoyed the play and it was amusing to see my class-mates performing. No doubt there were imperfections, but the audience clapped loudly. As Theseus said towards the end of the play:

The best in this kind are but shadows; and the worst are no worse if imagination amend them.

BOOKS AND LIBRARIES

When I was a child during the Great War and the 1920s few picture books for small children were published; nowadays the bookshops are crowded with coloured books of every shape and size – even books printed on thick cardboard for infants to chew and waterproof ones for the bath.

Remembered by my older sister Jean and me with nostalgia is an oblong illustrated book, *At War!,* published in 1917, illustrated and probably also written by Charlotte Schaller. This short piece of fiction, which was probably translated from the French, tells the story of a little French brother and sister living in Paris, whose father is at the Front; they, with their neighbours' children, played war games which always ended with the defeat of the wicked Germans (the

Boches). There were no good bookshops in Beverley and I think our father may have bought it for us on the way through London, coming home on leave from France. Like the children in the book, David, Jean and I also had a father in the trenches. We must have thumbed the book to pieces for it has long since disappeared.

After kindergarten days at Beverley High School I began to read on my own. Apart from a few moral tales, volumes which had survived from Victorian days, I enjoyed thumbing through some of the annuals which came our way. *Chatterbox*, an annual volume compiled from the pages of the magazine of the same name, was of great interest to Jean and me. With illustrations, some in colour, it was a fascinating farrago of fiction and non-fiction. In one of the early *Chatterbox* annuals, in 1922, a full-length story, in episodes, entitled *Jock of the Scots Brigade,* told the story of an eighteenth-century Scottish boy's search for his father who was a soldier in the Netherlands. This wonderful story has never been published as a separate novel, although other tales by the author, Alice A. Methley, have appeared.

One of the Victorian tales we both loved was *The Seven Golden Keys,* the adventures of Hilda, a small girl who searched for the keys in seven chapters. Another tale which impressed me deeply was a moral tale, *Joe Harman's Experiences*, in which Joe, who had emigrated earlier in the story, returns to England and is reunited with his long forgotten parents. I wept.

At school I was introduced to Charles Kingsley's *Water Babies* and, more appealing to me, his book *The Heroes, or Greek Tales for my Children (1856).* It was here that I heard first of Perseus, Theseus and the Argonauts. At Beverley Grammar School, to which I went at eight years old, we were soon introduced to Shakespeare in the watered down *Tales from Shakespeare* by Charles and Mary Lamb. One evening Dad asked me what I had to do for homework. 'We can do anything we like,' I replied. On further questioning he discovered that I had to write about *As You Like It.*

At home we had a copy of that beautiful edition of Robert Louis Stevenson's *The Child's Garden of Verses*, illustrated by Charles Robinson (John Lane, 1907). The fact that all three edges of this book glittered with real gold added to its attraction. Many of the poems had become family favourites with us; in particular: *My Shadow, The Lamplighter* and *Foreign Lands:*

> *I have a little shadow that goes in and out with me,*
> *And what can be the use of him is more than I can see . . .*

This was the favourite one of our little sister Betty. But in her haste to learn it she added words of her own, changing the second line to:

> *And what can be the use of him, I can see more than you can*
> *see.*

My own favourite was *The Lamplighter*, for we too had a street lamp outside the house to which the lamplighter came every evening with his ladder.

Among Dad's books were a number about the Great War, which he had luckily survived. He had bought a four-volume history of the war in which I found the illustrations of great interest. He also possessed several volumes of the post-war reprints of *The Wipers Times*, the newspaper which had circulated in the trenches. In it there were a couple of poems which Dad had contributed, one of them, *A Winter's Tale*, about snow being the perfect camouflage. He also had reprints of the old trench cartoons by the young officer, Captain Bruce Bairnsfather, which had originally appeared in the magazine *The Bystander*. I used to pore over the pictures of those veterans of the trenches, Old Bill and his companions. One of my favourites was the picture of Old Bill and one of his pals, their heads raised above a shell hole in which they were trapped. *Well, if you knows of a better 'ole go to it!* says Bill.

At the Beverley Public Library I was an avid reader. I cannot remember who introduced me to the novels of H. Rider Haggard; but I was soon an addict, not able to stop reading about the African adventures of Allan Quartermain and his friends. What wonderful characters they were! Umslopagas! Soon after Rider Haggard, I began to read the Tarzan novels by Edgar Rice Burroughs. After trekking with the dour Allan Quartermain, I was now swinging in the treetops with Tarzan. My sister Jean, always a witty verse-maker, composed an unflattering epitaph for me:

JIM
Here lies one who feared the soap,
One who lived in daily hope,
That an ape-man he might be
Swinging from the highest tree.

Sherlock Holmes followed close on the heels of Tarzan. Dad had several volumes of the short stories and an odd bound volume of *The Strand* magazine of the early part of the century. Brought up in Scotland by an uncle and aunt who had a printing shop and a newsagency in Newburgh, Fife, Dad had read all the early Sherlock Holmes stories when they first appeared in *The Strand* in the 1890s. This magazine was still going strong in the 1920s and Dad bought it every month. There I read some of the last Sherlock Holmes stories as they appeared.

The Librarian at Beverley, Mr Lockwood Huntley, had definite views about what children should read. I had heard of a book called *Dracula* by Bram Stoker. Not finding it on the shelves, I asked the Librarian. He told me that he had a copy but that I was too young to read it. However, my brother David, more than five years older than I, was able to borrow it for me. This story of Count Dracula, a Transylvanian vampire who comes to London seeking new blood, did not keep me awake at night.

It was when we were taught at the Grammar School by Willie Burrow, the English master, that most of us became serious readers. Willie sometimes, at the end of term, would read a short story, or an excerpt from a novel such as *The Cloister and the Hearth* by Charles Reade. He was a born actor who could reproduce the accents of characters in a story with ease. He introduced us to the short stories of Edgar Allan Poe and, in particular, I remember his recital of *The Cask of Amontillado* (especially the chilling last words of Fortunato: 'For the love of God, Montresor'). His rendering of Poe's *The Gold Bug* aroused my interest in cryptography. I soon found that the Beverley Public Library had a four-volume selected edition of his works, with suitable gloomy illustrations. My reading of them, including all his short stories, awakened an interest in Poe which has remained to this day. Before I left school I had avidly read his stories in which the Chevalier C. Auguste Dupin appears, *The Purloined Letter*, *The Murders in the Rue Morgue*, and *The Mystery of Marie Roget*, those splendid forerunners of the detective story.

Willie Burrow introduced us to most of the well-known English poets, demanding that we learn some poems by heart. Although never able to emulate my mother who learned by heart the whole of Macaulay's *How Horatius Kept the Bridge*, and never forgot it, even in old age; or her sister, our Aunt Florrie, who used to recite Robert Southey's poem about the wicked Bishop Hatto to her children during Zeppelin raids to divert their attention, and could still remember it in her nineties. But I did learn some poems which stay with me still; we memorised all the old familiar favourites: Wordsworth's *Daffodils* and *Upon Westminster Bridge*, Keats's *To Autumn* and parts of *The Eve of St. Agnes* and Coleridge's *The Rime of the Ancient Mariner*. Willie's recital of this poem was gripping and horrifying as he mouthed the words of the doomed sailor.

Another poem I remember well was Arthur Hugh Clough's *Say Not The Struggle Naught Availeth*. This short poem was probably inspired by the overthrow of the Roman Republic by Joseph Mazzini and is an inspiration to any minority group fighting a just cause. We heard more about Clough when our next English teacher, Norman Dawson, introduced us to Matthew Arnold's *Thyrsis*, a monody on the death of his great friend Clough.

It was first Willie Burrow and then Mr Dawson who started me on a life-long devotion to Shakespeare. At the age of fifteen, already an agnostic, although I did still attend the Baptist chapel every Sunday, for fear of offending my father, I used to take in my pocket a volume of

Shakespeare about the size of a hymn book. Sitting in a pew at the back of the church I would strain my eyes reading the small print of this multi-volume Victorian edition.

At home we had a well-illustrated set of the *Children's Encyclopaedia* (the Arthur Mee version), which I often read. There were also in the house several of the cheap sixpenny Woolworth's *Readers'Library*, abridged editions of the classic novels. Reading them I made acquaintance with Jonathan Swift's *Gulliver's Travels* and Defoe's *Robinson Crusoe*. The latter, which I had read many years earlier in a small abridged edition with fine coloured pictures, was, of all the books I read in my youth, my favourite book. It was closely followed by a small print edition of the *Arabian Nights*, probably the Lane translation, which I used to read under the bed-clothes with the aid of a torch.

Among my treasured anthologies is a little ink-stained book bearing my crude juvenile signature. It is *Golden Numbers: a book of verse for boys and girls*, selected and arranged by Mrs P.A.(Annie) Barnett, first published in 1906. Mine is the new impression of 1916. In it are many favourite, mostly narrative, poems, such as Rudyard Kipling's *The Ballad of the East and West*, Matthew Arnold's *The Forsaken Merman* (a poem that made my sister Jean weep) and the mysterious *Goblin Market* by Christina Rossetti.

In my last year at Beverley Grammar School, one of the set books we had to read for the English literature paper was that classic travel book by Alexander William Kinglake: *EOTHEN, or Traces of Travel brought Home from the East (1844)*. Kinglake was thirty-five when it was published, but the journey it describes, in lively fashion, was undertaken in his mid-twenties. Its evocation of what we now call the Middle East is unsurpassed. Of all its pages I loved the passage where he described a night at Tiberias, tormented by fleas:

> *No recent census had been taken when I was at Tiberias, but I know that the congregation of fleas which attended at my church alone must have been something enormous. It was a carnal, self-seeking congregation . . . devoted to the one object of having my blood. The fleas of all nations were there. The smug steady, importunate flea from Holywell Street; the pert, jumping puce from hungry France, the wary watchful puce with his poisoned stiletto; the vengeful pulga of Castile with his ugly knife; the German Floh with his knife and fork, insatiate, not rising from the table; whole swarms from all the Russias, and Asiatic hordes unnumbered – all these were there and all rejoiced in one great international feast . . .*
>
> *After passing a night like this you are glad to pick up the wretched remains of your body long, long before morning dawns. Your skin is scorched, your temples throb, your lips*

feel withered and dried, your burning eyeballs are screwed inwards against the brain. You have no hope but only in the saddle and the freshness of the morning air.

By devious ways my interest in books and literature led me to become a librarian. Although I have now been retired from librarianship nearly thirty years, I still haunt the libraries and bookshops and probably will continue so doing in the next life.

GILBERT AND SULLIVAN

Miss Morley, our elderly next-door neighbour in Norwood, must have thought she was seeing a ghost when I went to see her, dressed as a young girl in mid-Victorian costume and wearing a blonde wig. It was the day of the full dress-rehearsal of *The Pirates of Penzance* and I was one of the chorus of young maidens. That was in the days when I and all the other maidens had sweet treble voices. It was Mother who suggested that I should pop next door before making my way to the Assembly Hall near the Cottage Hospital. 'Miss Morley will be ever so surprised when she sees a little girl dressed as she was in the 1850s,' said Mother. For Miss Morley, now well on in her eighties, was born in the 1840s. Her front door was never locked, for she had difficulty rising from her chair and walking. When Nelly Good, her housekeeper, was out shopping, Miss Morley would often knock on the party wall with a special little wooden mallet. If Mother was busy she would ask one of us to go next door to see what she wanted. Often it was a trivial request; the truth was that the old lady was lonely. Occasionally she would press into my hand a sixpence which she withdrew from a small hand-knitted pence-jug. The coins were shining bright, for Miss Morley always washed the money that came from the bank or which Nelly returned to her when she came back from shopping. She was a doctor's daughter and a great believer in hygiene.

I was embarrassed to go next door dressed as a girl, so Mother came with me. Miss Morley peered at me and, leaning forward, felt the quality of my dress with her blue-veined old hands. Her eyesight was poor and I wondered whether she knew who I was and why I was dressed in that way.

In the 1920s, Mr Burrow and Mr Malkin, the music teacher, produced several Gilbert and Sullivan comic operas. Already there had been a production of *The Mikado*, in which my brother David appeared. His voice had broken, so he was chosen to be one of the Gentlemen of Japan. For weeks all the family had to listen to David singing the opening chorus again and again:

If you want to know who we are,
We are gentlemen of Japan:
On many a vase and jar –
On many a screen and fan,
We figure in lively paint:
Our attitude's queer and quaint –
You're wrong if you think it ain't, oh!

Next came *H.M.S. Pinafore*. By that time I was in the school choir, with a tolerable treble voice. Dressed in wigs and Victorian costumes my class-mates and I were to be the sisters, the cousins, and aunts of Sir Joseph Porter, the First Lord of the Admiralty, who was played by Mr Burrow. To my bitter disappointment I was thrown out of the chorus a week or two before the show for not singing loudly enough. I hid myself in the school lavatory and wept. The next year, I think it was in 1927, I managed to stay the course in *The Pirates of Penzance*, in which I was one of the numerous daughters of Major-General Stanley, a part played by Flemmy Rogers with great gusto. How familiar are the words and the melody even after more than seventy years!

Climbing over rocky mountain,
Skipping rivulet and fountain,
Passing where the willows quiver
By the ever-rolling river . . .

How we 'girls' rattled off the chattering chorus about the weather:

How beautifully blue the sky,
The glass is rising very high,
Continue fine I hope it may,
And yet it rained but yesterday,
Tomorrow it may pour again
(I hear the country wants some rain),
Yet people say, I know not why,
That we shall have a warm July.

Because it was sometimes difficult to find boys or masters to play the leading parts, the school imported gifted amateur singers from the town. One of them was my Aunt Doris, my Mother's youngest sister. In *The Pirates of Penzance* her rich contralto voice was well-suited to the role of Ruth, a Pirate Maid of all Work. In *H.M.S. Pinafore* she was Mrs Cripps (Little Buttercup), a Portsmouth bumboat woman. Expensive wigs and costumes were hired from London. We maidens in the chorus wore a mixture of blonde and brunette wigs as we flounced about the stage in our long mid-Victorian dresses.

The Pirates went down well with the audience, mostly made up of parents of the boys. Mr Malkin conducted the orchestra, which was composed of Beverley musicians from the town, plus a few gifted senior boys. In the middle of one of the choruses I was in the front row, only three feet from Mr Malkin's baton; suddenly I was horrified to hear him say in a loud voice: 'Sing up, Thirsk!' I was sure that the audience must have heard him; perhaps the make-up concealed my maiden blushes.

GRANDPA CHAPMAN

If you had been in Beverley Market Place several years after the Great War, perhaps in 1922, you might have seen an upright seventy-three year-old gentleman with a walking stick, neatly but not expensively dressed, with a small trimmed beard which showed signs of having been gingerish in its hey-day; he was about five feet and six inches in height, but looked taller because of the Homburg-type hat he wore. After forty years in Beverley Henry Chapman knew almost everybody he met in the town.

With his wife Damaris and three small girls all under five years, he had come to Beverley in 1882 from the Grimsby district of Lincolnshire. The opportunity to be a partner with Mr Botterill in a boot and shoe shop in the Market Place at Beverley was the reason for his move across the Humber to Yorkshire. The business was thriving, with employees in the workplace behind the shop, making boots and shoes to order. Before long, Mr Botterill retired; from then on Grandpa was the sole proprietor. As his family grew, the business prospered, until at its peak eleven men were employed. Before the end of the century more babies came, until the old family house in Lairgate housed eight girls and two boys.

Grandpa Chapman had endured and survived an unhappy childhood and boyhood. His mother, Martha Hall, the daughter of a wealthy farmer at Keelby in Lincolnshire, had eloped with one of her father's employees, Thomas Chapman, and was disowned by her parents. At first they prospered as tenant farmers at Bagmoor in Lincolnshire where they had three children; but at some time in the 1840s, for unknown reasons, and certainly before 1849 when Grandpa was born, in Winterton, near Bagmoor, their fortunes fell. By 1851 Martha and her children were living in Hull, in poverty, her husband having died of heart failure. Martha, in a poverty-stricken street near the docks, was described by the enumerator in the Census of 1851 as a pauper-seamstress. Martha then died, leaving Grandpa a baby of two, with two older brothers and a sister. Life in an orphanage from the age of two was not a good beginning, although Grandpa had no memory of better days. One of the skills he acquired at the orphanage was the art of boot-making and mending, which he put to good use in later life. At the time of his marriage to Damaris Lydia Goodhand, Henry Chapman was described as a merchant's clerk. As they were married in Grimsby, it is likely that he was working for a fish merchant.

With such a large family there had to be firm discipline. Grandma was too busy with housework, baking, cooking and bearing children, to be much involved with such matters. So Grandpa was the disciplinarian; his eight daughters in later life spoke of their father's strictness in their upbringing. But my Mother said he was more relaxed and even playful with his numerous grandchildren; and that is how I remember him. We children knew him much better than we knew Grandma. She was not as outgoing as Grandpa, seldom coming to see us, except when on a special visit with him. By contrast he was to us grandchildren always friendly and amusing. We knew him best after he had retired. At first he continued to live in the family home in Lairgate where he carried on the business with a couple of workmen. My sister Jean remembers calling to see him there at his bench. Without apparently having seen her, he greeted her before she could speak:

> *And how is Mistress Jean*
> *Have you been to see the Queen?*

Later they gave up the Lairgate house, moving to a small maisonette above a shop in Toll Gavel. But Grandpa could not bear to be idle. He had soon appropriated the ground-floor of a tiny abandoned cottage at the back of a shop. There he installed a bench and was soon happily mending shoes for the family.

One day he was on his way to our house in Norwood when he saw Jean leaving school. As she skipped along beside him, Grandpa started skipping. 'Don't skip Grandpa,' she said, fearing that the other girls would laugh at him. 'Why not?' he answered. 'If you can skip, so can I.' Inside Grandpa there was still a boy who often emerged with jokes, sayings and rhyming couplets. One day as I raced on my bicycle across the Market Place, probably dreaming that I was a Red Indian brave riding bareback, Grandpa, catching sight of me, immediately raised his walking stick to his shoulder and followed my progress. BANG! Another redskin bit the dust!

Grandpa often used to tap at our door and enter with a small wicker basket in which he had packed a few fresh eggs for Mother. He and Grandma loved their grandchildren, all twenty-six of them. They never saw the five children of their daughter Cissie, who lived in California, but frequent letters came, with photographs. Once, when I recited a poem at a concert in the Wesleyan Chapel during the Great War, Grandpa pulled out his leather purse and presented me with a sixpenny piece, which was a lot of money in those days.

Grandpa was a Methodist. A regular attender at the Wesleyan Chapel in Toll Gavel, he made sure that his eight girls and two boys attended chapel and Sunday-school. He also became choirmaster of the church in Toll Gavel, although I do not believe that he played the piano or any instrument. He had a clear tenor voice and his knowledge of hymns was extensive. But I never heard that he became a lay preacher or a deacon.

One of his amusing stories, which I heard many years later, was that Grandma, one rainy Wednesday evening, had braved the weather to attend the midweek prayer meeting at the chapel. She was the only person who turned up. According to Grandpa, the minister chose the hymn *Come O thou traveller unknown,* by Charles Wesley, based on the Bible story about Jacob wrestling with an angel.

> *Come, O thou traveller unknown,*
> *Whom still I hold, but cannot see;*
> *My company before is gone,*
> *And I am left alone with thee;*
> *With thee all night I mean to stay,*
> *And wrestle till the break of day.*

Saturday was a busy day in the Market Place at Beverley. The noise from the crowded market stalls, the stall keepers shouting their invitations to buy, the band of the Salvation Army and the general hubbub of the crowd, drowned all conversation. Grandpa said that one evening the Salvation Army preacher, raising his voice, cried out: 'What shall be our reward when we come to heaven?' From a vendor nearby came the answering cry: 'Peas all hot, peas all hot!'

On Easter Saturday, 1924, I had gone to see my cousin Geoff at their house behind a china shop in Toll Gavel. His mother, told us that our Grandpa was very ill and that he was sleeping. We had noticed that tan, made of the bark of trees, had been spread on the cobbles in Toll Gavel to deaden the sound of horses and carts, so that he would not be disturbed. This was usually done in Beverley when people were very ill. Grandpa had a cold which, after he had stood in the rain at the graveside of a friend, was followed by pneumonia. He was now in a coma. Auntie Florrie took us both upstairs to say goodbye to him in his bedroom. All we could see above the blanket was the small bearded head, with red cheeks and forehead, breathing slowly and loudly. He died the next day in his seventy-fifth year.

In his delirium, some of his daughters heard him struggling to say the words: *Rivers of water, rivers of water.* Was this perhaps a cry for water from a man with a raging temperature; or was it that, dreaming of a Paradise to come, he was remembering one of the Psalms he knew so well?

> *And he shall be like a tree planted by the rivers of water, That bringeth forth his fruit in his season; His leaf also shall not wither; And whatsoever he doeth shall prosper.*

TWO INDIAN POLICEMEN

It was probably in 1929 that my school friend Noll and I, both about fifteen years old, decided that we would join the Indian police when we left school. Whose idea it was I do not remember. I had already some time before had ambitions to become a policeman in this country, preferably a plain-clothes detective at Scotland Yard. I was to be the greatest sleuth of them all, Sherlock Holmes included. Dad knew a police sergeant who lived near us in Beverley and one evening took me along to his house. The Sergeant spoke of the long hours on the beat, the slowness of promotion and the poor pay. He mentioned that I would have to be at least 5 ft 9 inches tall and even taller in the Hull City police. All this dampened my enthusiasm, for I was only 5 ft 6 inches and not likely to gain more than an inch or two. Detective work obviously wasn't easy and crimes were not solved by sitting in an armchair, like Sherlock, smoking a pipe. The kind Sergeant lent me a dozen copies of a police magazine to read at home, but after reading them I decided that the police force in this country was not for me. But the Indian police – here was my future!

My friend Noll and I must have seen an India Office advertisement seeking applications from suitable men to join the Indian police. I had written for details and application forms. The fat buff envelope marked O.H.M.S. arrived one summer morning in 1929. It was cricket day in the afternoon so I took the documents to school so that Noll and I could study them when we were waiting our turn to bat.

There were two hurdles. Firstly you had to be physically fit at nineteen years old, which was the minimum age for applications. We were sure that this could be achieved in the four years we had to prepare. The second requirement was that you had to sit for a special Civil Service written examination; sample question-papers were available. A language course in Hindi had to be taken before embarkation.

I already knew a little about India from my Aunt Annie Chapman, a nurse who had been working there as a Methodist medical missionary since 1919. During her first return home she told many stories about her life in Akbarpur and Benares and even taught us a few phrases in Hindi. Her work was sometimes with the Untouchables. She had met Gandhi once when one of his followers asked if they could stay a night in the courtyard of the hospital where Aunt Annie was the matron. Noll and I studied every word of the India Office documents. We became familiar with all the perks of the job, including a monthly allowance in rupees for the maintenance of our horses. For days we argued about the job and how we would spend our time after leaving school, preparing for the great day.

One of our problems was how to become fit enough to pass the medical tests which came before the written examination. Neither of us was keen on sports or physical training. However, I had recently purchased by mail order a book about a system of physical training known as Maxalding. For this I paid 10 shillings in monthly instalments of 2 shillings and sixpence. The system preferred muscle flexing and stretching instead of physical jerks. Suppleness rather than muscle building was the key to success, they said. Noll studied the book and we both decided that we could achieve the necessary fitness by the age of nineteen.

Fortunately for us these dreams of becoming Indian policemen on horseback faded. Otherwise we might have been given the job of arresting Gandhi.

PRIZEGIVING DAY

We all looked forward to Prizegiving Day, a day free of lessons. It was the 'swots' who swept up most of the prizes – books of their own choice, embossed with the school coat of arms and motto and signed on a label inside by the Headmaster himself.

Most of us enjoyed it for the spectacle. It wasn't every day that all the masters donned their best gowns, decorated in the colours representing their colleges and universities. The Mayor of Beverley, wearing his chain of office, his Mayoress and an attendant bearing the town mace added to the solemnity of the occasion. Some of us, especially in the later years at school, found the spectacle amusing and sometimes uproariously funny.

As it was impossible to hold the Prizegiving in the cramped quarters of Beverley Grammar School, the school hall of the Wesleyan Chapel in Toll Gavel was hired for the day. Pupils sat at the front and parents at the back of the hall. The gallery provided extra seats for parents. The masters sat at the back of the platform, wearing their best gowns. The ceremony began with the entrance of the Mayor, the masters and the Headmaster. On the table in front of the Mayor stood the prizes, a mountain of books.

The Mayor himself conducted the programme, which usually began with a song by the school choir, which stood at the left of the platform. A memorable year was when one Bob Wood, a well-known local character, was Mayor. With his broad East Riding accent and loud voice he announced the titles of the song. 'The choir will now render *'Oo is Sylvia?'* he boomed. Bob Wood did not worry about losing the sound H at the beginning of words or adding it to others; he spoke the English language just as his forebears in Beverley had spoken it. In a speech he made he urged us all to study hard. 'I believe in heddication,' he told us.

Paddy Burden always made a speech after the Mayor. We all clapped heartily after each event, pleased to be able to make as much noise as possible. The school choir sang many songs, mostly the well-known English folk or traditional ones. Interspersed were poems recited by boys who had good voices. Usually stirring and patriotic ones were chosen, such as Henry Newbolt's *He Fell Among Thieves:*

> *Ye have robbed, said he, ye have slaughtered and made an end,*
> *Take your ill-gotten plunder, and bury the dead:*
> *What will ye more of your guest and sometime friend?*
> *'Blood for our blood,' they said . . .*

Another favourite was the same author's poem *Drake's Drum:*

> *Take my drum to England, hang it by the shore,*
> *Strike it when your powder's running low;*
> *If the Dons sight Devon, I'll quit the port of Heaven,*
> *And drum them up the Channel as we drummed them long ago . . .*

On opposite walls of the Wesleyan Hall hung two very large framed photographs of a man and a woman. The man was my Uncle Clem, one of my mother's younger brothers, who was serving in Burma as a Wesleyan missionary. The other one was Annie Chapman, one of Mother's younger sisters, a medical missionary in India, who had trained in England to be a nurse and was now in Benares. Both of them had the large spade-like chins which they had inherited from their Grandmother, Lydia Suddaby. One year at the Prizegiving, proud of being related, I nudged my neighbour and, pointing to one of the photographs, said, 'That's my Uncle.' My reputation for kidding and practical jokes was well known and he didn't believe me. But, thinking it funny anyway, he passed the news to his neighbour. So it went on down the seated row of my classmates. A little while later I nudged him again, pointing to the other portrait: 'And that's my Aunt.' Chuckling at what he thought was my joke, he passed the message on: 'And that one's Thirsk's Aunt.' The whole class rocked with suppressed laughter. Nobody believed me.

The boys who were to receive prizes mounted the platform when they were called, collected book or books, shook hands with the Mayor and the Headmaster and returned to their seats. I collected only two prizes, one in the first year at school and the second in the last year: *Blackie's Boys' Annual* and Edgar Allan Poe's *Tales of Mystery and Imagination.* The latter was the leather-bound Everyman edition which I still have.

The ceremony ended on a solemn note with the singing of the national anthem and the school song. We all stood stiffly to attention as we implored God to save our sovereign King George V. We all relaxed as we sang the school song:

Forty years on when afar and asunder,
Parted are those who are singing today . . .

FOOD OF THE GODS

Jack Skinner was one of my best friends at school. We both enjoyed the same sort of jokes and laughed at the predicaments of school life. He had a nimble wit and was never downcast.

Sometimes after school I would cycle with him to his home in Willow Grove, overlooking part of the Westwood. Jack had a small steam-engine that he would fill up with water and light the methylated spirit burner. When we had seen enough of that we would go to the large warehouse behind the house. Jack's father was a wholesale grocer who supplied many of the shops in Beverley and district.

The warehouse was full of sacks of raisins, sultanas, currants and other dried fruit. These were not sold in packets; they were delivered to the shops in sacks which Mr Skinner's man would take by horse and cart to the retail grocers. There were many boxes of tinned foods of all kinds. Biscuits were sealed in large square tins that were delivered in this form to the grocers.

The warehouse was an Aladdin's cave for us. We would climb up to the warehouse ceiling, treading on sacks of sugar, rice, flour and dried fruits until we reached the top. On the way Jack would extract a tin of sardines from a box and a handful of raisins that had spilled out of a sack. Comfortably perched on sacks out of sight beneath the rafters, we would enjoy the feast, eating the sardines in our fingers. At that time sardine tins had a metal key which you rolled around the tab at the end of the tin and turned. The beer-can type of ring used nowadays on tins was unknown. George the warehouse man was fond of Jack and he turned a blind eye on our feasts.

I cannot remember having any drink to wash down this delectable food. Cans of drinks were a later development and I do not remember seeing bottles of lemonade or ginger beer there. Mr Skinner probably could not compete with Mr Straker, a manufacturer of bottled lemonade and other fizzy drinks, at a small factory in Lairgate.

This Mr Straker also had a son who was in my class at school. Sometimes after school I would cycle with him to the factory. The men would allow us to watch them working. Those who were putting the gas into the already-filled glass bottles wore protective spectacles, in case a bottle shattered. They then inserted a glass marble or 'Ally,' which sealed the bottle-neck. You had to have a special tool to open one of these bottles. It was a hollow cylinder capped at one end and with a 'prodder' at the other. To open a bottle you placed this implement over the neck of the bottle and pressed hard. The ally descended into the cavity below but it did not stop the flow of drink as you poured. I do not remember being offered a sample of any of the drinks made in the Straker factory.

SEVENTY-THREE NORWOOD

Soon after Dad came back from the Great War in 1919, Mother and he realised that the house in St Mary's Terrace was too small. Betty, our little sister, was born that summer and Mother found the lack of a bathroom like the one in Ryde Street, Hull, where we had lived until the Zeppelin raids began, was a great handicap. An earth-closet in the garden made life difficult with four children.

The possibility of returning to Hull was considered. This would be more convenient for Dad, whose job as a Customs officer was at an office near Queen's Dock; on the other hand, David, Jean and I were settled at schools in Beverley. So when Mother heard of a larger house in Norwood which was available for rent, they decided to move. Dad would have to continue to commute; not a great hardship, for the train journey from Beverley to Hull was only about fifteen minutes and it was less than ten minutes to the station on foot.

It was not until 1921 that we moved. Born in Hull just before the war, I had no memory of the move to Beverley; but I remember this move. It was an exciting prospect and I was curious about the house in Norwood. I had not been taken to see it when Dad and Mother had been shown around by the landlord; but one Sunday before the move, Mother said I could go on my own to look at the outside of number 73. As I stood on the pavement opposite, I was impressed by the height of the building, which seemed enormous compared with our house in St Mary's Terrace.

Motor pantechnicon vans were not known in Beverley at that time; our removal vehicle was a horse-drawn open cart. With all the furniture aboard, I was allowed to sit by the driver; but where was Mother? Did she also ride on the cart? Or did she walk behind? The house we were going to was less than a mile from St Mary's Terrace. As we passed the High School in Norwood, I felt happy that I was riding on a cart loaded with furniture while my fellow-pupils were busy in the kindergarten.

The house was twice as large as our old house; it stood in Norwood in the middle of a row of five imposing houses, known as Lorne Terrace. The front room looked out on to a small garden. At the back of the house, a long narrow garden, with brick walls on either side, ended with a gate at the bottom, leading to a communal footpath along the back of the five houses; on the path stood an ancient water pump, still active, from which we could draw jugs of pure cold water, much better than the tap water in the house. Our Uncle Jim, the Waterworks Manager, took a sample for analysis and pronounced it pure and safe to drink.

In the bathroom, which had a large bath but curiously no hand-basin, stood an imposing Victorian or possibly Edwardian water-closet mounted on a dais, like a throne. The stairs were wide, with polished hand-rails designed for sliding down. My bedroom was the large front attic; from its dormer window I had a bird's eye view of all the passing traffic and the activities of the neighbours.

The house was lit by gas and there was a gas cooker. In addition, an old-fashioned kitchen range had an oven on the left of the fire, in which Mother often baked bread ; also a boiler for water which was heated by the fire. The tall fireguard with its polished brass rail, which I had known so well in the past, came with us to Norwood.

A plum tree at the end of the garden was ideal for climbing. From the top, with a good view of the next-door garden and beyond, I could repeat Robert Louis Stevenson's experience as a boy, told in his poem *Foreign Lands*; only his was a cherry tree.

Up into the cherry tree
Who should climb but little me?
I held the trunk with both my hands
And looked abroad on foreign lands.

I saw the next door garden lie,
Adorned with flowers before my eye,
And many pleasant places more,
That I had never seen before . . .

In September when we came back from holidays at Brid, the Victoria plums were ripe; what a delight it was to climb the tree and eat the biggest one you could find.

Dad soon set about brightening the house by painting over all the wallpaper. Under the bay window in the front room he built a wooden window-seat. Mother made cushions and curtains which hid compartments under the seat. Each of us children had a private compartment in which to keep toys and books.

It was a happy home, and there we lived through the rest of the 1920s and all through my schooldays, which ended in 1930.

MUSIC WITH MALKIN

For most of us at Beverley Grammar School the weekly music lesson was enjoyable; it was also a welcome break from the monotony of some of the other subjects. Mr Malkin, the music teacher, was the organist at St Mary's Church, Beverley, his job at our school being only part-time. He was a mild man, whose face had a permanent look of resignation. 'Bug-whiskers' was the name he had been given by our predecessors and the name stuck throughout the eight years I was at the school. Schoolboy nicknames for their teachers are sometimes cruel, but in this case it was affectionately given, solely I suspect, because of the small moustache he had grown.

With Mr Malkin we sang our way through the whole repertoire of English traditional songs and all the other old favourites, including such stirring Welsh and Scottish songs as *Men of Harlech* and *The Campbells are Coming*. Strangest of all were the national anthems. At some time in the nineteenth century, probably in the 1890s, a former music teacher had acquired twenty or thirty copies of a publication with the title *National anthems of the world*. Over the years we must have been through those dog-eared copies many times. We knew the words of most of them in the English translations given, but when we came to *La Marseillaise* we sang it in our best French with great gusto:

> *Allons enfants de la patrie,*
> *Le jour de gloire est arrivé...*

Among my favourites were the anthems of Belgium, that of old Russia and the Serbian. The most popular of all was without doubt the Japanese anthem, partly because of its haunting melody and partly because we could pretend that we knew the Japanese language, by mouthing the phonetic rendering which appeared above the English translation:

> *Ki mi ga yo wa*
> *Chi yo ni ya chi yo ni*
> *Sa za re i shi no*
> *I wo to na rite*
> *Ko ke no mu su ma de*

I discovered that on our old piano at home I could play this strange melody using the black keys only. I have read that the music was composed by court musicians in 1880. The words are said to date from the 9th century A.D. The translation by Sakuzo Takada is:

> *May thy peaceful reign last long!*
> *May it last for thousands of years*
> *Until this tiny stone will grow into a massive rock*
> *And the moss will cover it all deep and thick.*

Those of us who were in the school choir all had reasonably good treble voices and we could sing in tune. Yet only a handful of boys who were learning the piano, or some instrument privately, could read music. Mr Malkin spoke occasionally of quavers and demi-semi-quavers, but few of us were interested or knew what he was talking about. Our ignorance of the history of music was appalling. We were never told about the great composers and we had few opportunities to hear their works. Nevertheless, my class-mates could sing, except for three or four out of thirty, who, because of their raucous voices, similar to that of Mr Punch, were excused music lessons. They were known as the non-singers.

Every day at morning assembly, which was attended by the whole school and all the masters, we sang hymns, accompanied by a senior boy who was a gifted pianist. After eight years of singing we must have gone through most of *Hymns Ancient and Modern* several times. We had our favourites of course and *Onward Christian Soldiers* was one of the best. Pa Ross, the ancient French master, had a powerful voice which, with a hymn like that, became *fortissimo*. As he sang, his face became redder and redder; and, at the end of the hymn, his monocle would fall from his eye with dramatic effect. Ikey Simpson, the French master who succeeded Pa Ross, sang no hymns and looked uncomfortable throughout morning assembly. At the end of term, when we sang *God save the King*, Ikey stood with his arms crossed over his chest, while the rest of the school stood stiffly to attention. Was he a republican, we wondered? And an agnostic?

FORTY YEARS ON!

Another song which we sang only at the end of each term, on Speech Day, or on special occasions, was *Forty years on*. This well-known school song was originally written for Harrow School by one of the masters there, Mr Edward Ernest Bowen; it has been adopted by many schools since 1872 when it was first written. The music was composed by a colleague at Harrow, John Farmer. Here is the full text, which is seldom seen in print. At school we only sang the first and the last verse.

> *Forty years on when afar and asunder*
> *Parted are those who are singing today,*
> *When you look back and forgetfully wonder*
> *What you were like in your work and your play.*
> *Then it may be there will often come o'er you*

Glimpses of notes like the catch of a song.
Visions of boyhood shall float them before you,
Echoes of dreamland shall bear them along.

Follow up! Follow up! Follow up!
Follow up! Follow up! Follow up!
Till the fields ring again and again,
With the tramp of the twenty-two men.
Follow up! Follow up!

Routs and discomfitures, rushes and rallies,
Bases attempted, and rescued and won,
Strife without anger, and art without malice –
How will it seem to you forty years on?
Then, you will say, not a feverish minute
Strained the weak heart and the wavering knee,
Never the battle raged hottest, but in it,
Neither the last nor the faintest, were we!
Follow up, etc.

O the great days, in the distance enchanted,
Days of fresh air, in the rain and the sun,
How we rejoiced as we struggled and panted –
Hardly believable forty years on!
How we discoursed of them, one with another,
Auguring triumph, or balancing fate,
Loved the ally with the heart of a brother,
Hated the foe with a playing at hate!
Follow up, etc.

Forty years on, growing older and older,
Shorter in wind, as in memory long,
Feeble of foot and rheumatic of shoulder,
What will it help you that once you were strong?
God gives us bases to guard or beleaguer
Games to play out, whether earnest or fun,
Fights for the fearless and goals for the eager,
Twenty and thirty and forty years on.
Follow up,etc.

After the final morning assembly of the school-year Paddy Burden made speeches and said nice things about the boys who were about to go out into the real world. Then we sang the school song. A boy named Constable had a rich fruity voice and his job each year was to sing solo the final *Follow up!* As we began the last verse, *Forty years on, growing older and older,* the pianist seemed to introduce a sombre feeling to the melody, perhaps echoing the thoughts of some of the older masters who were nearing retirement. As for me, I couldn't help smiling one year when I caught sight of my friend and class-mate Jack Skinner, always the wag, surreptitiously hunching his shoulders in imitation of a decrepit old man.

In 1997, an old boy of Beverley Grammar School, Peter Nicholson, who had been a pupil at the school during the Second World War, from 1939 to 1944, wrote a witty last verse for the old school song. It was printed in the *Beverley Advertiser*:

> *Fifty years on and still getting older,*
> *Leaking and creaking and things going wrong;*
> *Hair disappearing and feet getting colder,*
> *With several spare parts that were made in Hong Kong.*
> *But we're still in contention and still could take prizes,*
> *At talking and yawning we'd win every year.*
> *But perhaps we should mention our greatest surprise is*
> *To wake in the morning and find we're still here!*
> *Follow up, etc.*

BIKING DAYS

It wasn't that I crept to school unwillingly like Shakespeare's snail. My problem was that I could not get out of bed, especially on cold mornings. Mother used to call me again and again, 'You'll be late for school, Jimmy!' And I usually was, which meant that I suffered far too many half-hour detentions after school. These gave you plenty of time for meditation, for you sat completely still at a desk with the other delinquents, arms folded, silent and without moving a muscle.

Beverley Grammar School was on the other side of the town from where we lived at number 73 Norwood. It was just under one and a half miles away and I reckoned that I could pedal there in seven to ten minutes, depending on weather conditions. Most of the way it was flat, with only a slight rise in the last lap up Queensgate, approaching the school.

In the 1920s most of the bicycles were without gears and those that had them only had three, the famous Sturmey-Archer kind. When I started at the Grammar School in 1922 at the age of eight Dad ordered a bicycle from a shop in Hull; it had to be made, for small bikes of this kind were not available off the peg. When we received a postcard telling us the bike was ready, Mother took me into Hull to collect it. We managed to stow it on a bus after much argument with the conductor. I had been practising in the back garden on an old bike my sister used, designed for females, without a bar. The only difficulty I had was that I could not mount. For the first few weeks at my new school I had to prop the bike against a fence or a wall and push myself forward. Dismounting caused me no trouble. Before long I was leaping on to the saddle like a cowboy.

My journey was down Norwood, up Hengate, past St. Mary's Church, whose accurate clock face warned me whether I was late and must pedal faster. Speeding along North Bar Within and Lairgate, I was soon turning right into Keldgate; then Queensgate and school. In the 1920s there was no way except by Lairgate and Keldgate because you had to cycle along two sides of the Admiral Walker Estate, consisting of a large mansion and many acres of grassland, occupied by a fine herd of Highland cattle, with shaggy hides and long horns. In the later twenties after the old Admiral died, a road was built across the grassland, through a forest of new houses which the Council built. It shortened the journey to school, but I was often late, as before. Where did the Highland cattle end their days?

In the 1920s motor cars were a rarity, a majority of the vehicles being the horses and carts of the carriers and tradesmen. One day Mother was in the town shopping when she saw a horse and cart coming from Lairgate into North Bar Within, with hay overhanging both sides. From underneath the hay I emerged on my bike. 'There was plenty of room,' I said, when Mother cautioned me. Cycling was safe except on race days. These were two days in June when streams of horse-drawn wagonettes loaded with punters came through the town from Hull; there were also loaded motor charabancs. I had to cross the stream of cars and buses, wagonettes and those on foot, slowly moving along North Bar Within on their way to the race-course on the Westwood. Those two days in the year were full of excitement. Posters would appear on walls of the town: **'Beware of pickpockets!'**

It was safe to leave bikes outside shops or in the bike sheds at school without locking them. One summer evening I had cycled about a hundred yards to Miss Wild's sweet shop in Norwood. My bike and I went everywhere together. I had gone to bed and was nearly asleep when Dad called up to my bedroom: 'Where's your bike?' Usually we kept them in the front garden and only brought them in at night. My mind raced. I suddenly realised what I'd done. 'Oh, it's outside Miss Wild's,' I shouted, much alarmed. Dad walked along and found it still there.

Cycling through snow was difficult when it was thick on the ground. Nowadays motor-cars flatten it quickly, but it took ages to disappear at that time. My friend Noll, whose home was in Walkington, a village some three miles west of Beverley, had greater woes in winter. The journey down to school, descending from the Wolds, was an easy one, freewheeling most of the way down through the Westwood. The journey back, even in the best of weather, was a gruelling task, especially on a bike without gears. On dark winter nights, with flickering oil lamp, he claimed that he heard loud shrieks as he pedalled past the mental hospital. Another boy, Grayburn, from Leven, a village about six miles east of the town, had a smooth flat ride, but one winter morning I saw him covered from head to toe with snow as he passed our house.

For a period of a year or so I had to walk to school, return home for dinner and go back again at 2 p.m. My first bike was too small for me and a new bike could not be afforded. I used to study the Raleigh catalogue with great interest until at last the day came when Dad said I could choose a new one. That it had no gears did not worry me, for most of my cycling was in and around Beverley or to the east where it was flat. The price was £5-19s-6d.

In my walking days to school, Sam Elder, who was in my class, sometimes gave me a lift on his bike, with me standing on the back-step. This useful piece of metal sticking out from the back hub, is not, I think, fitted to modern bikes; its original purpose was to help you to mount the bicycle. My friend Tom Barry's father, a perpetual curate at the Minster, used to mount his ancient bike in this way, wobbling dangerously. Sam would try to dislodge me by swerving from side to side. At the junction of Keldgate and Lairgate, coming back to school in the afternoon, I had to get off Sam's bike and walk the rest of the way. For one of the many school rules, read out at morning assembly once every term, forbade any boy giving a lift on his bike to any other boy between the end of Keldgate and the school. It was I think on my first day at school that I disobeyed the rule. My brother David, only about fourteen at the time, gave me a lift on his bar, because my new bike had not yet arrived. As he cycled along Queensgate, one of the prefects, on foot, pulled him up and told him off. Fortunately this transgression was not reported to the Headmaster.

A bike was a great blessing in Beverley; it was easy to jump on your bike and visit school friends at the other side of the town in a few minutes. About half a dozen of us ganged up together; after school we would cycle to each others' houses or go further afield to explore some of the secret places of the Westwood, such as Burton Bushes, an ancient remnant of the forest which at one time covered the whole area. My brother David explored every street in Beverley on his bike. Once he made a list of all the public houses in the town, He claimed that there were more pubs to the population than anywhere else in the kingdom.

PUNCH AND JUDY ON THE BEACH

One of the best things I looked forward to at Bridlington, where we usually went for our holiday every September in the 1920s, was the Punch and Judy show. Every year it was there on the sands, no matter whether there was scorching sun or that cold east wind that blows from the North Sea. 'Bright breezy bracing Brid,' they used to say.

For me the show was a magnet. I could watch for hours this strange story of Mr Punch's crimes, from battering his baby until the final scene when he kills the Devil. Never were there so many corpses in half-an-hour. I loved Mr Punch, with his raucous voice, large hooked nose, curved chin and hump on back. What a rascal he was, and how we all cheered when he hanged the hangman! 'What a pity, what a pity!' he would cry as he placed the corpses in a row on the shelf. 'That's the way to do it,' he squawked.

I was about eleven years old when the idea came to me that I could have a Punch and Judy show at home. I had for some time tried to amuse my young sister Betty by manipulating some of her dolls and animals from behind the settee. My brother David, more than five years older than I, said he would make me a full-sized Punch and Judy booth. It worked after a fashion, but David was no carpenter; his contraption, made out of old pieces of timber, wobbled and threatened to collapse.

Dad came to the rescue. He had already made us a full-sized square beach tent which we took on the train to Brid every year. Now he bought suitable timber and made a collapsible framework around which mother stitched together a light canvas covering. On top of the structure was a removable proscenium, with curtains and a ledge for the puppets. Inside, another ledge served to keep the puppets ready to hand.

All was ready, except for the puppets. Sister Jean made a Mr Punch, painting his hooked nose, chin and hump on cloth to make a figure which was filled with straw. With his red velvet hat and cloak, Mr Punch was ready for action! By this time Betty, knowing the dialogue almost as well as I did, was able to help by standing beside me in the booth and handing me the appropriate puppet on cue. Although I kept mainly to the traditional dialogue, I also introduced some scenes of my own invention. One of these episodes was a boxing match between African Sam and Grappling Gorilla, using two of Betty's dolls.

At first I gave shows only to the family or to friends and relations who came to our house and who were patient enough to watch. But news spread and soon I was asked to perform at a Boy Scout concert held in the schoolroom of the Baptist Chapel. This meant collapsing the booth and trundling it from our house to the chapel, loaded on one of our bikes.

I do not remember being nervous or embarrassed when giving a performance, partly I think because I was concealed from the audience; but when the show ended, instead of emerging to take a bow, I moved the whole booth off the stage, with me inside. I knew the dialogue well, but, compared with the show on Bridlington sands, I am sure that my production was a pale imitation. With my voice still unbroken I could imitate the nasal twang of Mr Punch; but it was not the authentic sound, which can only be produced with the aid of the professional swazzle, held in the mouth. Amateurs are warned about the danger of swallowing this device. In the profession there is a tradition that you must swallow your swazzle three times before you can call yourself a real Punch and Judy man.

Nowadays some local authorities have attempted to ban Punch and Judy shows on the grounds that the drama is not suitable for the ears of young children. But you have only to look at the faces in an audience of small children and hear the laughter to know that Mr Punch is not dead yet.

On top of the books on my desk Mr Punch sits now, his red velvet hat somewhat threadbare and without the stick with which he had vanquished so many. My booth and all the other puppets have long since disappeared!

> Mr Punch is a jolly good fellow
> His dress is all scarlet and yellow . . .
> He lives, while he can, upon clover;
> When he dies – it's only all over . . .

I wish I had known about a service which took place in May 1962, commemorating the 300th birthday of Mr Punch. It was held at St Paul's Church, in Soho, London. Nearly fifty Punch and Judy showmen turned up, most of them with their own Mr Punch. Canon Clarence May preached the sermon, holding a Mr Punch in his arms. During the service the bark of a dog was heard. 'Is that Dog Toby?' asked the Canon. Afterwards, surrounded by the booths of many showmen, one of the venerable Mr Punches pulled a golden cord, to reveal a tablet on the wall of the church portico, which reads:

> 'Near this spot Punch's puppet show was first performed in England, and witnessed by Samuel Pepys, 1662.'

GOING TO CHAPEL

My grandfather, an unpaid pastor of the Scotch Baptist Church in Beverley, had three sons, including my father, all of whom were lay preachers and deacons in the Baptist Church. My other grandfather was the choirmaster of the Wesleyan Chapel. With all this holiness on both sides of the family you would have thought that some of it would have rubbed off on me.

In my earliest days at Sunday School I listened intently to the words of my teacher, Miss Edith Arnott. I believed every word she spoke. When collection time came, we sang as we placed our pennies in the glass jar with its wooden slotted lid:

> *Hear the pennies dropping,*
> *Listen as they fall,*
> *Every one for Jesus*
> *He shall have them all.*

I took the last line literally, believing that all the money was sent to that kind bearded man with flowing cloak, surrounded by children of all colours, whose picture hung on the wall of the schoolroom.

As time went by I became a young sceptic; how this happened I cannot now remember. Looking back, I find it strange that Dad, devout as he was, never pressed me to take more interest in Sunday School or chapel. It is true that I continued to attend both, until I was about seventeen, partly from fear of censure by Dad if I made a sudden break. My older sister Jean was persuaded to become a Sunday School teacher, but I cleverly avoided this by offering to become the Secretary, whose job was to keep the attendance record. Sitting at a desk I checked the names of the scholars as they arrived.

In chapel I moved from the family pew to a small pew at the back corner of the chapel, where I could read my little volumes of Shakespeare, which were about the size of a hymn book. The elderly widow of one of Dad's ninety first cousins always sat in our family pew; she often turned towards me with a glance of approval at my seemingly devout studies.

After some time it was announced that an organ-blower was required. I jumped at the opportunity. The ancient organ, built long before electricity was installed, was powered by hand. In a tiny room to the left of the organ a wooden lever like a pump handle had to be moved up and down vigorously as soon as a hymn was announced. A long weighted piece of string indicated that pressure must be kept above a certain line on the wall. It was an easy job to keep the bellows inflated and I could continue reading my Shakespeare between hymns. Only once did I let the organist down. Trying to read at the same time as pumping, I allowed the weight on the string to fall below the mark. The hymn-tune began to die with a wailing sound, as when a bagpiper fails to blow enough air into his bag; but it was soon brought to life again after I had pumped furiously.

Dad never insisted that I should be baptised; in fact the subject was never raised. In the Baptist church baptism usually took place when you were in your late teens. Below the pulpit was a large bath formed from marble slabs, with steps leading down to the water. When the time came, several candidates would don bathing costumes, over which they wore a white sheet. The bath was filled earlier in the day, with a kettle or two of hot water to take the chill away. The parson, wearing similar garb, then descended into the water, completely immersing the candidates one by one. So, unlike my great-grandfather Thirsk, who, according to the parish register, was baptised twice, once as a baby in 1792 and again at four years (presumably the first one had not taken), I remain unbaptised.

One of the happiest memories of chapel was the women's sewing party on Wednesday afternoons, which ended with a groaning table full of sandwiches, plum bread, scones, teacakes, rock cakes and all the other ingredients of a Yorkshire tea, made by the members. On such days Mother used to say: 'Come straight to chapel, Jimmy, when you leave school.' I didn't need reminding.

When at seventeen I wrote to the Baptist minister resigning from my job as secretary of the Sunday School, I decided also to cease going to chapel on Sundays. Dad never made any comment on my break with religion. I remember overhearing him saying to a friend: 'Jim will have to find his own way to salvation.'

At the Grammar School the new English master, Mr Dawson, was also required to teach Divinity once a week to the combined classes V and V-Upper. He was an agnostic who, probably without Paddy, the Headmaster's, permission, began to tell us about other religions. His lessons were an eye-opener to all of us and we began to learn that, in the big world outside, Christianity with all its sects was only one among many religions. Decades later, when I corresponded with Mr Dawson, I asked him if he remembered the Divinity lessons. He wrote back, recalling that he had been carpeted by Paddy:

> *because of a complaint by a parent that I had spoken lightly of the devil. The parent (a missioner to seamen in Hull) said the devil was still a potent force in the world. But there was a twinkle in Paddy's eye when I told him I would not again take the devil's name in vain. Looking back, and seeing what I have seen of the world since then, I think there was a case to be made for the indignant parent!*

From the library I was borrowing and reading avidly volume after volume of the works of Anatole France, in English translation, in that orange-backed series which was published in the 1920s. These were some of the books and influences which led me down the road to agnosticism and humanism.

ENTERTAINING PARSONS

Whenever the parson at our Baptist chapel was ill or on holiday or had resigned, Dad, as Secretary of the church, in consultation with the other deacons, had to find a temporary substitute. Sometimes it would be a missionary on home leave, glad to earn a pound or two, sometimes a parson temporarily without a church and occasionally a young student newly qualified, from the Rawden Baptist College.

Unless these relief parsons lived locally a bed for the night had to be found. We took more than our share of hospitality, partly because Dad was the Secretary and partly because Mother didn't mind the extra work looking after a visitor.

We four children were warned beforehand. 'You must be on your best behaviour when the Reverend X is staying,' said Mother. 'No rude remarks at meal-times and no laughing.' But it was difficult for us because almost always the visiting parson had some peculiarity of appearance or of voice or of habits. It was often impossible for David, Jean and me to suppress our mirth; even Betty, much younger than us, often saw the joke.

Mother was not good at remembering surnames. 'For heaven's sake try to get his name right,' said Dad. But Mother often got it wrong. When Trevor Quick stayed a weekend with us, she several times called him Swift. 'Now, Mr Swift, would you like some more potatoes?' You could almost hear Dad's suppressed groan. On another occasion we gave hospitality to the Reverend Craven. 'Oh, I'll remember his name,' said Mother, 'I'll think of the cigarettes: CRAVEN A.' 'Well, make sure you do,' said Dad, 'and don't forget and call him Mr Woodbine.'

Sometimes the visitor had an unusual name. One of them, a female minister, proudly bore the name Georgette Bloomer. It was as well that she did not come to our house, but was given hospitality by three stalwart pillars of the church, the Misses Arnott, three maiden ladies who lived in North Bar Without.

One, a tall man whose name I forget, wore a frock-coat. After the morning service he strolled across the garden with Dad while Mother prepared the Yorkshire pudding. Glancing out of the window Mother spotted me following behind the minister, gazing at his coat-tails. She called me in. 'Jimmy, what on earth are you doing?' she asked. 'I was only trying to see where he put his gloves,' I replied. 'He seems to have a secret pocket in the tail of his jacket.' Mr Owen Clover was a missionary, on leave from Africa. After dinner he retired to his room and returned with a piece of tapestry. 'Oh, how beautiful!,' said Mother. 'Is that done by the natives?' 'Certainly not,' said Mr Clover, 'It's my own work, I take it with me wherever I go.'

Before Mr Clover left on Monday morning he asked Mother if there was a nursery or a flower shop in Beverley. She directed him to Backhouse's in North Bar Without and he returned with an enormous bunch of gladioli. Mother, thinking that he wanted to take them home for his wife, placed them in a bucket of water by the front door. As he was saying goodbye, he noticed them and said: 'Haven't you any vases you could put them in?' 'Oh,' said Mother, 'I was keeping them fresh so that they wouldn't wilt on the journey.' 'They are for you, Mrs Thirsk,' said the parson.

Mr Wilson was not a parson, but occasionally he came to the Baptist Chapel to talk about the work of a home for the orphaned children of seamen, of which he was the Secretary. One of their homes was in nearby Hull so he did not have to stay the night with us. After several visits for meals we knew him well. When, during the mealtime on his first visit, Mother offered him the salt and pepper pots, he refused with the words: 'I thank you, no; I take no condiments. I only use salt to clean my teeth.' And smiling broadly, he revealed his large white teeth. Mother could see that we were nearly killing ourselves trying to suppress our laughter. 'Next time he comes,' said Mother, 'you must not ask him if he would like the condiments.' But the next time he came, either Mother herself forgot her warning, or, more likely, deliberately asked Mr Wilson, 'Will you have the condiments?' He replied as before and we could not fully repress our laughter; nor could Mother. 'I'll get some more gravy from the kitchen,' she said, seizing the gravy boat and retreating.

Some of these hilarious episodes passed over Betty's head. She was, however, a keen observer of the habits and peculiarities of the visitors. To have a permanent record she sized them all up after they departed and awarded them stars, according to how well she liked them.

It was rare for a visiting minister to have a car; they had to be met at the railway station and escorted back at the end of the weekend. One who did have a car was our Uncle Clem, one of Mother's younger brothers. Although a Methodist – he was a missionary who had spent a large part of his life in Burma – he occasionally preached at our Baptist chapel when visiting Beverley. Uncle Clem possessed a second-hand De Dion-Bouton, a French car of pre-Great War vintage, of which he was very proud. A more recent car he had buried in his garden at Mandalay when he fled the country on the approach of the Japanese in World War II. He escaped on foot with many of his flock, reaching India after many privations. He never knew whether the Japanese found his car.

When I now look back at the procession of ministers throughout the 1920s, I cannot help thinking that it was Mother who bore the main burden of the hospitality. All those Yorkshire puddings, those joints of beef, those vegetables; all those makings of beds, washing of sheets, the endless cups of tea. Yes, Mother was the heroine.

A RUNAWAY MULE

At least twice during the 1920s a battalion of the Territorial Army came to Beverley Westwood on the occasion of their summer camp. I believe they came from the West Riding but I cannot remember of which regiment. They erected their tents on the grassland to the south of the Walkington Road below the Anti-Mill, which is now the golf-house. This alien invasion had a great fascination for us boys. We had a cadet force at the Grammar School, but I was not a member. With other curious boys I would cycle up to the camp in the evening to gaze at the strange army life enjoyed or endured by hundreds of men in uniform.

Only once did I see them on a route march. It was during school holidays. I was at home one morning when I heard the sound of a band. Dashing up to my attic window I looked out to see a whole battalion of men marching along Norwood, heading towards Hornsea. The officers on horseback were followed by the ranks of soldiers, marching four abreast, shouldering their Lee-Enfield rifles. The gun carriages, drawn by horses or mules, followed. The column was headed by the band, playing well-known marching tunes such as *Colonel Bogey, Pack Up Your Troubles* and *Old Comrades*. I did not have any ambition to be a soldier; but when I cycled to the Westwood to see their camp, I was fascinated at the sight of so many soldiers.

One summer evening I had cycled up to the camp to have another look at army life. Suddenly a large mule, drawing a gun-carriage, startled by some incident, began to bolt. Reaching the road near the camp, with the ashen-faced driver tugging at the reins without success, it started galloping down towards Beverley, the carriage swaying from side to side. Two or three of us leapt on our bikes and, by pedalling fast downhill, we were just able to keep up. Down Cartwright Lane they hurtled and on to Keldgate. I began to wonder what would happen when they came to the Minster, for there the road turns sharp left towards the town. The young soldier held on when the carriage swerved into Eastgate. By this time a local off-duty policeman had joined the chase on his bicycle. The gun carriage crossed Wednesday Market, but it was clear that the poor beast was now exhausted. When the policeman saw that the mule had come to a slow trot after galloping so far, he cycled past it, dropped his bicycle on the pavement about twenty yards ahead in Lord Roberts Road, and as the mule came level, ran alongside, seizing hold of the shaft with one hand and the bridle with the other. By pulling hard he stopped further movement. The mule, covered with sweat and with foaming mouth, stood trembling while the young soldier stepped into the road, also trembling.

I hope that the young soldier was not punished; but, knowing the army, I expect that he would have been placed under arrest as soon as he returned to camp. A dozen years later he and many of his comrades who were still on the reserve would have died in France or have been waiting to be rescued from the beaches of Dunkirk in May 1940.

BOY SCOUTS

I became a Boy Scout at about the age of thirteen. My cousin Geoff, a year older than I, joined at the same time. The troop was sponsored by the Baptist Church in Lord Roberts Road, Beverley; our meetings were held in the schoolroom of the chapel.

At the first meeting we were measured for uniforms by Mr Peabody, a local gents' outfitter who was a member of the church. Special care was taken with our head measurements to ensure that the Canadian Mounties style wide-brimmed hat was a good fit. There was great excitement when, a few weeks later, the uniforms and equipment arrived. Thanks to Mr Peabody the appearance of the troop was satisfactory; every Scout had his lanyard and a whistle, his scarf with a toggle to keep it in position and his scout pole. The latter was like a broomstick; in fact I probably bought mine from Briggs and Powell, the hardware shop in the Market Place. To disguise its whiteness I quickly carved strange patterns at the top, with painted, coloured rings down the length of it.

The troop was large enough to be split into patrols; cousin Geoff and I were in the Cobra Patrol. To identify ourselves in the dark to other members of our patrol we imitated what we imagined was the hiss of the cobra. Fortunately none of us had ever met a cobra even in a zoo, so we never really knew whether our hissing sounds were authentic.

One of our first lessons was on the Morse code and semaphore methods of communication. The Morse code is fairly easy to learn, but it is difficult to become fluent. Practising with torches in the dark and with one flag on a stick in daylight, we improved weekly. Semaphore communication was more difficult to master. Using two flags, or sometimes using the arms only, it was possible to pass messages at long distances if you had good sight.

Another skill we learned was the art of knots. We only practised tying about a dozen or so of the thousands illustrated in the book. The reef knot and the useless granny knot most of us knew already; but we were soon learning how to tie slip knots, knots for tying together two pieces of rope of different thicknesses and how to tell the difference between a sheepshank and a sheet bend.

Mr Campey, our Scoutmaster, was a clerk working for the East Riding County Council. He was a quiet efficient leader, never raising his voice or losing his temper. His brother, who assisted him, was by contrast a keen physical fitness man who had formidable muscles, acquired in his job at the Beverley shipyard.

We all read the book *Scouting for Boys*, written and illustrated by the founder of the Scout movement, the soldier Baden-Powell; I have never forgotten his illustration of how to remedy a dislocated shoulder by placing one foot in the casualty's armpit and pulling hard. A St John's Ambulance man who was called in to give us lessons on first-aid and how to apply splints and bandages told us never to use this drastic method on a shoulder.

We knew the heroic story of the siege of Mafeking during the Boer War, when Baden-Powell held on for 217 days. He had founded the Scouts before the Great War and, by the time of the international Jamboree in 1920, it had become a world movement. Our troop obtained permission to attend another Jamboree in York in 1927. Hiring a truck, we were driven to York to join the thousands of scouts from all over the world, many of them camping in tents on the York racecourse. We didn't stay the night, but we had time to go to the service held at York Minster. To our astonishment, as we entered the Minster in single file, there at the door to greet us was Sir Robert Baden-Powell himself, a tired-looking old man of seventy years, wearing Scout uniform and with bare knees. He smiled at each of us wanly as we passed him within three feet. What a day we had! We were now able to say we had seen the Chief Scout in the flesh! He died in Kenya in 1941 during World War II, as Baron Baden-Powell.

Another publication which I read avidly was *The Scout*, the magazine which came out on Thursdays each week. On the way to school I called to buy my copy from Mr Holmes, the newsagent at the corner of North Bar Within and Hengate. I had devised a method of propping *The Scout* on the handlebar of my bike, so that at least I could sample some of the articles and stories before I got to school. One serial particularly interested me; it told of the adventures of Frank Darrell, a private investigator, who was able to disguise himself quickly in an emergency. Also included were regular articles of great interest to us boys, such as the art of tracking animals and hints on camping.

Our first camp was for a weekend only, with tents pitched in a field belonging to the Manor at Lockington. For most of us it was our first night sleeping outside a house. I forgot my knife, fork and spoon, but Mother, finding them after we had set off, jumped on her bike, cycling six or seven miles from Beverley to Lockington. To save my embarrassment she left the cutlery at a lodge at the entrance, where a woman said she would take them up to our camp. A memorable time was when we camped for a whole week at Atwick, on the East Yorkshire coast near Hornsea. Much of our time there was occupied with the slaughter, with a tent peg mallet, of a large number of black beetles which had invaded our tents. Sing-songs round a camp fire while quaffing rich cocoa, diluted with condensed milk, were a great delight.

Among the camp fire songs, which were for the most part traditional, such as the *Grand Old Duke of York*, we sang more popular songs such as: *Yes, We Have No Bananas*. But the most popular song of all was *The Woad Song* which we sang with great gusto to the tune of *Men of Harlech*. Because it seldom appears in print, here is the full version. Woad is a plant from which a blue dye is produced. The ancient Britons daubed this on their bodies.. The reference to Butcher Row is to the Beverley shop of Mr Peabody, the gents' outfitter. In the original it is Savile Row in London, home of many famous tailors:

THE WOAD SONG

What's the use of wearing braces,
Vests and pants and boots with laces?
Hats and spats you buy in places
Down in Butcher Row.
What's the use of shirts of cotton,
Studs that always get forgotten?
These affairs are simply rotten:
Better far is woad!

Woad's the stuff to show, men,
Woad to scare your foemen!
Boil it to a brilliant blue,
And rub it on your back and your abdomen.
Ancient Britons never hit on
Anything as good as woad to fit on,
Neck or knees or where you sit on.
Tailors you be blowed!

Romans came across the Channel
All wrapped up in tin and flannel.
Half a pint of woad per man'll
Dress us more than these
Sax-ons you can waste your stitches
Building beds for bugs in breeches.
Not a nest for fleas.

Romans keep your armours
Saxons your pyjamas
Hairy coats were meant for goats
Gorillas, yaks, retriever dogs and llamas.
Tramp up Snowden with your woad on
Never mind if you get rained or blowed on
Never need a button sewed on
Go it, ancient Bs!

The words were written by Mr W. Hope Jones, a mathematics master at Eton.

Boy Scouts are unarmed and I suppose that nowadays they are not allowed to carry a sheath knife or any kind of a knife. Most of us carried a large folding knife, with one stout blade and a spiked piece of pointed metal, which we were told was for removing stones from a horse's hooves. Several of my fellow-scouts possessed sheath knives, but I did not. At home, however, I had a villainous-looking, hand-made hunting knife whose nine-inch ancient blade was housed in a hand-made sheath. This was a gift from my Aunt Annie, the medical missionary in India who had asked what present I would like from India when she came home on leave. She had bought it for a few annas in a bazaar at Benares. I also had a deadly knife with beaded coloured handle and scabbard, given to me by my Uncle Clem, a missionary in Burma.

The Westwood at Beverley was a wonderful training-ground for Scouts. There we could play a version of hide and seek, with one patrol as the hunted ones, another as the hunters. Once among the trees you could hide until the cows came home. Other activities on the Westwood included estimating the height of the Black Mill, using our Scout poles and the length of the shadows. We also practised semaphore signalling with flags. To cover long distances quickly on foot we used Scout's pace. To do this, you ran twenty paces, followed by twenty paces walking quickly; by running and walking alternately in this way it was possible to move quickly without becoming exhausted. Other 'trade secrets' we gleaned from reading Baden-Powell's own book *Scouting for Boys* and from the *The Scout*.

We all attempted to pass tests for the various badges which could be sewn on our shirts to show how good we were. The cook's badge was a popular one. I passed it by cooking a meat stew in a pan on a fire I had built in a lane near our house. The Scoutmaster came to inspect and taste the meal when I had finished. The cycling badge, which I passed, involved knowledge of the working of the bike, mending punctures, adjusting brakes, and a demonstration of safe cycling. This was one of the easier badges.

After two years of Scouting some of us began to weaken; we had sampled all the activities and we were beginning to be weary of repeating what we had done already. Other activities beckoned as we grew older; I had become interested in table tennis and had joined a local club. In the summer evenings when homework was done I preferred bowling at the nets at the Norwood cricket ground to scouting on the Westwood. In the dark days of winter I liked to stay at home reading my books.

Several of my fellow Scouts were of a like mind; so, after chewing the matter over at length, we told the Scoutmaster that we wished to leave.

TOM BARRY

Tom Barry, who also lived in Norwood, Beverley, less than one hundred yards from our house, was a madcap. There was no other word for him. He was the son of an elderly white-bearded Perpetual Curate at Beverley Minster. I cannot believe that his father's salary in such a job amounted to much; but his wife, who was much younger, may have had her own income. Tom had generous weekly pocket money, which never stayed in his pocket long.

Tom was a boarder at a school in the seaside town of Bridlington. He was a boisterous lad; had he been at home all the year he would have disrupted the household and disturbed the meditations of his father, a mild little man who could not have survived the gale of Tom's presence for long. It must have been bad enough for the old man during the school holidays.

As in the case of many friendships, I cannot remember how I first met Tom; he had no brothers, but his older sister Vivien was a fellow-pupil of my sister Jean at the High School for Girls. Mother had a nodding acquaintance with Mrs Barry, who may have invited me to the house one day during the school holidays to play with Tom. However it happened, we were soon close friends who saw a lot of each other when he was home from school.

We were completely different in character. Tom was the boy of action. I was the dreamer. I would suggest some new adventure and Tom had the energy to organise everything that was necessary before we embarked on a project. One example of this was when we set up a detective agency. I had been greatly influenced by a private detective named Frank Darrell, 'the man with many faces,' whose adventures appeared weekly in the 1920s in *The Scout*. I was an avid reader of this magazine, being at that time a Boy Scout myself. The idea of the detective agency appealed to Tom, who found a small suitcase to hold the equipment we would need. A bunch of old keys became skeleton keys. We manufactured false beards and moustaches. Tom had an air-pistol and an old tobacco tin full of lead pellets; he also had a camera. We had notebooks and pencils with which to record the number plates of the few passing motor-cars which we saw occasionally on country roads near Beverley. We both of course had electric torches, mine being one you could change from white to red or green. With this suitcase strapped on the rear carrier of Tom's bicycle we would set off for a half-day's sleuthing, cycling along country roads. Back home at the Barry house we would play in the garden until the maid brought out our tea on a tray. The first time I tasted Marmite sandwiches was there.

One summer we decided to become actors. Tom and I immediately cycled down to see Mr Goldthorpe, the chemist, from whom Tom bought several sticks of greasepaint in a variety of colours. One of the plays we had put together must have been concocted around a Dr Fu-Man-Chu story, for we painted our faces yellow with long drooping black moustaches. We invited Mrs Barry and her daughter Vivien to see the performance. One day we had to adjourn for our midday meal, so rather than take off all the make-up I ran home along Norwood in my Chinese garb, startling Mother as I sat down at the table.

At the Barry house Tom had appropriated one of the rooms for himself. It was an extension to the house, built on stilts. To enter it you had to move a panel from the bathroom wall, descending a couple of steps into a large rectangular room. Tom had a train set, with the tracks permanently fixed to the floor. We spent many happy hours in this 'secret' den.

We went into business. I had come across a recipe for making Carron oil, which at that time was one of the remedies for treating burns. The recipe was simple: a mixture of linseed oil and lime water. These two ingredients were shaken together in a bottle. The labels we made ourselves. I seem to remember that we sold at least two bottles, one to my family and one to Tom's.

A more alarming chemical experiment led to disaster. Mr and Mrs Barry had moved to a house near the sub-post office in Norwood. Tom was sad to lose his room on stilts where the train set lived. But in the new house was a garden shed with a bench, which Tom appropriated. Next door to it was a chicken run and another wooden hut to which the chickens retired at night. In the hut Tom had a variety of bottles containing chemicals, including sulphuric and hydrochloric acids. He loved experimenting with the production of small rockets. We also tried devising tricks, such as the conversion of one liquid to another of a different colour. I remember in this connection the use of logwood chips. All these chemicals Tom bought from Mr Goldthorpe. He also bought cigarettes which we puffed occasionally.

Disaster came when I put a half-smoked cigarette on the bench where it became soaked in acid. Tom gave me another cigarette and threw the soaked one into a rubbish bin in the corner of the hut. Shortly afterwards Tom and I cycled off, probably to the shop to buy more cigarettes. When we returned half-an-hour later, the hut was on fire. Neighbours were in the back garden passing down buckets of water which Mr Dobbs, the neighbour from the sub-post office, threw on the fire. Someone suggested calling the fire brigade, so Tom and I pedalled furiously to the nearest telephone box. I remember him lifting the telephone and shouting FIRE! But the fire engine never came and I think it was likely that the girl at the telephone exchange thought it was a hoax call. We returned to the fire which by this time Mr Dobbs had almost quelled. Several chickens had been rescued but the corpses of a few with singed feathers were visible. The chicken hut and Tom's hut were both completely destroyed.

We convinced our parents that a bottle of acid had fallen off a shelf and ignited the contents of the rubbish bin. Fortunately nobody suspected that we both smoked cigarettes.

Often we would roam around Beverley Westwood, where in one of the woodland parts known as the Lime Kilns we found a tree which high up had what we called 'The Crow's Nest' in which we could sit quite comfortably and talk. One of the holes of the golf course was beyond the trees; the golfers had to drive a ball high above the wood, trusting that it would land somewhere near the flag on the next green. Sometimes we heard the hiss of the balls above our tree, but many of the golfers failed to clear the wood and had to root among the trees for their lost balls, unaware that up above their heads we sat, watching their failures to find their balls.

As we came to the end of schooldays both of us found other interests. The days of make-believe were gone. Tom bought a drum-set, joining in with a new friend who played a saxophone. He also set up a photographic business in a rented room in Beverley. I suspect that his mother paid the rent, for there was little custom. His next venture was a petrol station about a mile north of the town. There he mended bicycles, sold petrol and carried out minor motor repairs. I visited him there several times and he was always pleased to see me. I never knew what became of Tom during World War II. After the war I heard that he was a woodwork teacher at a school in the north of England.

A SUMMER DAY

One of my best friends at Beverley Grammar School was Raymond Oliver, who lived in the village of Walkington, about three miles west of Beverley. His was a strange history. Conceived in America in the state of Washington, where his mother had gone to marry a Yorkshireman who had emigrated earlier, Raymond contrived to be born in England in the City of York, where he first went to school. To him York was holy ground; to the end of his days it remained the greatest city in the world.

His father was christened Oliver Cromwell Oliver, a name suggested by a devotee of the Lord Protector who had been consulted about the naming of the boy. He emigrated to America in the 1890s, where in California, after unsuccessful attempts to find gold, he had taken a job with a railroad company, laying new track. He had no training in engineering, but had a good eye for planning the best route for a railway. It was thirsty work for Oliver Cromwell Oliver, who developed a love of strong drink which remained for the rest of his life.

In 1914 Raymond's mother hurried from America to her home in York, determined that her first child should be born in England. The Great War began on 4th August 1914, a few weeks after Raymond was born. Soon afterwards his father came back to volunteer for the Army, in which he served for the remainder of the war. In France he found a job he knew well, laying new railway tracks for the trains bringing men and munitions to the front.

Raymond's home in Walkington, where the family moved when his father returned from the war, was named Cromwell Abbey by some local wag because part of some ancient stonework had been incorporated in the front face of the building. The best part of the property was at the back of the house where several acres of land were occupied by fruit trees and vegetables. Mr and Mrs Oliver, Raymond and his two younger sisters looked after these, picking the fruit when it was ripe. Mr Oliver had no regular job, but managed to survive the 1920s and 1930s by selling fruit and vegetables and by digging gravel from a nearby quarry for a local builder.

Raymond was known at school as Noll, named by Willie Burrow, the English master, after the joking epitaph for Oliver Goldsmith, suggested by the actor David Garrick:

Here lies Nolly Goldsmith, for shortness called Noll,
Who wrote like an angel, but talked like poor Poll.

One memorable sunny summer day in 1927 I cycled across the Westwood to Walkington to see Noll, who had already spent an hour digging gravel to help his father. He had recently bought a second-hand air-rifle, which, although it didn't have telescopic sights, was reasonably accurate. Noll had obtained lead shot from Akrill's, the gunsmith in Beverley market place. How often had I gazed longingly at a Webley air pistol in their window!

Through the orchard we tramped, to a narrow clearing of grassland beyond the apple trees, not far from the boundary of the property. Noll had brought several empty tin cans from the house and the stump of a candle. These we set up on the ground about thirty feet away, with the lighted candle on one of the tins. We fired first from a prone position, taking turns. The noonday sun warmed the backs of our heads as we continued firing. Before long the tins were well peppered and we both managed to snuff the candle occasionally. It was a blissful time. Afterwards we ate sandwiches, followed by several rather tart, not quite ripe apples.

In the afternoon we talked about the famous athletes of the day. Neither Noll nor I took part in any of the school sports except cross-country running, football and cricket, which were compulsory. But we both had a great interest in reading about the famous athletes of the day. At that time Paavo Nurmi, 'the Flying Finn,' was breaking world records. There were stories in the papers about his long training runs across the Finnish countryside, stop-watch in hand. Primo Carnero, the giant Italian boxer, nearly seven feet tall, was often in the news. We measured his height on the shed behind the house and marvelled at the accounts of a man who ate a whole bunch of bananas after his main meal.

Noll told me some of the stories his father loved to tell about his roving days in America before the Great War. Once when entering a saloon and passing through the swing doors, he brushed shoulders with a man who was leaving. Arriving at the bar Noll's father was mystified that nobody spoke a word. A man standing next to him at the bar asked 'Do you know whose shoulder you brushed as you came in? It was Frank James, the outlaw, older brother of Jesse James.'

On another occasion Noll's father had seen the memorable fight between the black boxer Jack Johnson and the Englishmen Bob Fitzsimmons at Philadelphia in 1907. Fitzsimmons, originally a blacksmith from Cornwall, was a powerful man just under six feet tall. By the time he met Jack Johnson he was 44, fifteen years older than his opponent. Johnson, the son of a black slave, was a Texan, who later became the heavyweight champion of the world. But on this occasion he was knocked out by Bob Fitzsimmons.

So ended a long happy summer day filled with good talk about the things that interested us and friendly rivalry firing his air-gun.

Some seventy years later Noll and I were talking one day about our schooldays. 'Do you remember when I cycled to Walkington to spend the day with you?' I said. 'We went shooting with your old air rifle.'

'Yes,' said Noll, 'I do; and that practice with the air-gun came in useful and profitable later. I was called up in 1940 in the Green Howards. At the end of three months' infantry training my platoon was due to go to the firing range. All thirty of us agreed that we would put twopence each in the kitty and the man with the best score would get the lot. Well, I finished with a good score, easily the best in our platoon. So I scooped the whole five bob, which I spent on beer that evening in the local pub.'

'That's amazing,' I said and I told him my story. Almost the same thing had happened to me. At the end of infantry training in the King's Own Royal Regiment we were about to go to the firing-range when our platoon sergeant said he would give five shillings to the man who got the top score in the platoon. So off we went, with our ancient Great War Lee-Enfield rifles (mine was dated 1917) to see what we could do. 'Imagine my joy when I saw the results pinned up on the board outside the Company office,' I said to Noll. 'I came third in the whole company and had the best score in our platoon. Most of the platoon congratulated me, one of them pulling my leg and telling me I would be made a sniper before long. After several days somebody asked me whether the sergeant had paid me the five bob. I told him that I hadn't received a penny. Unknown to me he told the rest of the lads, who promptly each contributed twopence. So I got my five shillings in spite of the sergeant's broken promise.'

FIRST LESSONS IN CRYPTOGRAPHY

Mr Morris was Dad's best friend. Both of them were officers in His Majesty's Customs and Excise service in Hull; both of them had volunteered in 1914 and they had served in France, although not in the same battalion, throughout the Great War.

After the war, Mr Morris was living alone near Hull. His wife had died in childbirth during the war when he was in France. The baby had also died. Their adopted son was brought up in a children's home. Mr Morris was a frequent visitor to our house, especially on summer evenings when he would arrive on his motorbike. Dad and he had long sessions together revising for a Customs examination which would allow them to progress to the rank of surveyors.

Mr Morris was fond of us children; he often brought little presents and asked us conundrums. One day a letter came from him, addressed to me and my older sister Jean. We were completely baffled, for the whole letter was a jumble of typed letters of the alphabet. About ten lines of this weird letter filled the sheet of paper; some of the 'words' only had two or three letters, while others were longer with four, five or even six letters. The first line was:

og upi vsm dpzbr yjod vtuayphtsq o eozz rsy qu jsy

We thought it must be some kind of code, but there was no way we could unravel the mystery.

The next time Mr Morris came over to Beverley, he asked us: 'Have you been able to read my letter?' ' No,' we replied, 'we couldn't make head or tail of it.' 'Find me a large sheet of foolscap paper,' he said, 'and I'll show you how to make sense of it.' First of all he wrote all the letters of the alphabet, in order, down the left-hand side of the paper. Then he counted how many Ts there were in the message, how many Hs, and so on. When he had been through the whole message, he said: 'Now look, both of you, which letter in the message appears more often than any other?' We could see that there were more Rs than any other letter. The next letter which had appeared most frequently was letter Y. When we had placed them all in order, Mr Morris said: 'The most common letter in English words is the letter E, the second most common is T. So let's start by writing E on top of every letter R in the message. Then T over all the letter Ys.' Jean noticed that one of the three-letter words now had E at the beginning and T at the end. 'That must be EAT' she said, 'I can't think of any other word that would fit.' 'Right,' said Mr Morris 'and now you've found that S is A, fill in all the Ss with an A. Gradually the message began to look like something we could read. I spotted a three-letter word that could only mean CAN, and soon we had the complete message in front of us. The first line was:

IF YOU CAN SOLVE THIS CRYPTOGRAM I WILL EAT MY HAT

'Now I'll show you how I wrote the message in cipher,' said Mr M. I typed it on my typewriter at home, but instead of typing the correct letter I typed the letter on its right. So instead of typing E, I typed R, the one on the right of E on the keyboard.' It all became clear once he had explained it. Then he told us that we could vary the message by hitting the typewriter key to the left of the letter instead of to the right. Or we could hit the key two places to the right or left. As long as the person to whom we were sending the secret message knew which way we had done it, he or she would be able to decipher it. Dad had a small portable Corona typewriter, so we were able to type our secret messages. We sent a letter in cipher to Mr Morris, but he solved it very quickly. Dad said that Mr M. had been a battalion intelligence officer during the war.

Years later, Willie Burrow, our English master, read to us Edgar Allan Poe's short story *The Gold Bug*. In it the method of solving a simple substitution cipher was clearly explained, using the same method which Mr Morris had shown us in the early 1920s.

During the Second World War I was on leave at home one day when Mr Morris telephoned Dad. Passing the phone to me Dad said: 'Have a word with your old friend Mr Morris, Jim.' We exchanged a few words. 'I hear that you're in the Intelligence Corps now, Jim,' he said. 'I won't ask you what you're doing, because I know that you can't tell me.'

Remembering how he had introduced us to cryptographic messages in our childhood, I was longing to tell him that I was now working at the Headquarters of the Government Code and Cipher School at Bletchley Park. I was never able to tell him or my father what I had been doing during the war, because the secrets of Bletchley Park were not generally known until 1974, after they had both died.

NEARBY SHOPS

Several shops in Beverley were close to our house in Norwood. Of all these, that belonging to the Misses Petch remains clearest in memory. It was almost opposite our house, standing on the corner of Norwood and Mill Lane. The Petch sisters and their brother, who seemed old people to us children, were probably in their fifties. The younger sister, rather stout, looked after the shop; the other, Laura, the lean one, managed the household and looked after their brother Jim, who was not married. Jim had a few cows in a field nearby; he also kept some hens, grew vegetables and kept bees in old-fashioned skeps. Laura was very deaf, which was probably why she did not serve often in the shop. I remember standing in the shop and hearing Jim's loud voice shouting from the back room: 'Is me shirt ironed, Laura?' One morning my sister Jean popped over to the shop to get something for Mother. A smell of frying bacon met her as she opened the door. In a loud voice from the rear Jim was telling Laura: 'A'll hev another rasher an some bred an' dip while yer on, Laura.'

A stranger entering their shop might well think that he had been transported back in time a hundred years, so little had changed in this old-fashioned general store, where you could buy most of the household goods and food required to sustain life. Firewood, string, treacle, salt, tinned fruit and fish, Dolly blue and lemonade – all these and many others were arranged higgledy-piggledy, although the sisters knew the location of everything. The bundles of firewood, housed underneath one of the bay windows, were difficult to reach; the stouter Miss Petch was always pleased if you retrieved a bundle for her. Treacle was in an ancient metal container with a lever at the bottom. When Mother said: 'Slip over to Petch's and get me some treacle, Jimmy. Here's a clean jam-jar,' I would place the jar under the tap while Miss Petch and I waited until it filled. In winter this process proved incredibly slow, as we watched and waited. Jean too has memories of the firewood and the treacle and adds to the list boxes of candles, gas-mantles (for those who lit their houses with gas), muslin-wrapped hams hanging from hooks on the ceiling, mops, brushes, and zinc buckets. Boxes of sewing-threads were all on wooden bobbins that came in useful if you were doing French knitting. Jean also noticed that Miss Petch had an unusual method of storing her ten shilling and £1 notes. £5 notes were seldom seen. Coins, from half-crowns and florins down to farthings, were all dropped into separate compartments in the till. But notes were stuffed, apparently at random, between the boxes and tins that lined the shelves behind the counter. 'I have thought since,' said Jean, 'that it might have been Miss Petch's security plan.' In autumn Jean remembers that Jim Petch would bring into the shop baskets of Victoria plums and their attendant wasps.

Round the corner in Mill Lane, next door to the Petch's shop was what must have been the smallest cobbler's shop in England. Hardly more than the width of the door, it was probably an outbuilding of the Petch's. The shop consisted of a counter behind which the cobbler mended the boots and shoes. Before we moved to Norwood all our boots and shoes were mended by Grandpa Chapman, Mother's father, who had retired from his boot and shoe shop in the Market Place at the end of the Great War.

The cobbler in Mill Lane, who mended our shoes after Grandpa died, was deaf and dumb. He had perhaps learnt the trade at an orphanage, like Grandpa in earlier days. As you walked down Mill Lane, passing his shop, you could see him, behind his bench, hammering away. He seemed to be a contented man who always had a smile for his customers; but the only sound that ever came from his mouth was a kind of grunt, as if he was trying to talk to you.

Mother in her youth had learned the deaf and dumb alphabet, where I do not know. She could spell words on her hands and fingers, letter by letter, and although she taught me the letters, at my request, I could never spell out the words as quickly as Mother. When she asked me to take a pair of shoes for mending, I was able tell him what was required. As I slowly spelled out on my fingers the words, 'Sole and heel, please', the cobbler would nod his head vigorously and grunt through a mouthful of nails, which he took out one by one, as he hammered them in. Years later, in her old age, Mother was in a hospital ward, recovering from a broken ankle. The nurses and doctors were having difficulty communicating with a deaf and dumb woman who was in the same ward. Mother came to her rescue by acting as interpreter.

A short distance down Mill Lane on the right, was another corner shop, that of Mrs Brindle. It was also a general grocery store which Mother occasionally used. Mrs Brindle always had a large Yorkshire ham on the counter from which she carved thin lean slices by hand. Most of our groceries were delivered by Mr Baggs from his shop in the market place, but Mother liked to use all the local shops from time to time.

Mr and Mrs Dobbs had a grocery shop and sub-post office further up Norwood, not more than 60 yards from our house. I could sprint there in a matter of seconds when Mother asked me to buy half a pound of butter. Both Mr and Mrs Dobbs ran the post office and the shop efficiently, but usually it was Mrs Dobbs who looked after the grocery department.

The sweet-shop of Miss Wild stood lower in Norwood, almost opposite the entrance to the cricket ground. It was there that I usually spent my 6d pocket money every Saturday. It was enough to buy a bottle of Vimto, a fizzy brown liquid of uncertain origin, a twopenny bar of Fry's chocolate cream, twenty aniseed balls and a packet of Smith's crisps with a pinch of salt wrapped in blue paper inside. With these in hand I would spend the afternoon watching the cricket. Entrance to the cricket ground was free for those who, like me, had an annual pass which had cost my Dad five shillings. The price included practice any evening at batting or bowling at the nets.

Much nearer into the town, on the left, almost opposite Norwood House, Mr Abbott had his pork-butcher's shop. In the window were displayed all the products of the pig, from trotters to a pig's head. One of his specialities was potted meat covered with melted butter. His pork pies and his brawn were also popular.

One winter day Mother called at the shop, probably to buy potted meat for tea, which, spread on bread and butter, was one of our favourites. Mr Abbott was complaining of the cold: 'It's my hands, Mrs Thirsk, they never get warm all day long, handling the meat on marble slabs.' 'Oh,' said Mother, trying to be helpful: 'You should rub your hands through your hair, that's what I do when my fingers are frozen.' At the moment Mother spoke, she realised that Mr Abbott was as bald as a coot!

THE BEES

Soon after we moved to Norwood Dad decided to keep bees. Nobody in his own family had ever taken up beekeeping, but his younger sister Margaret was married to a Scotsman, our Uncle Tim McQuisten, who had a few hives. He had persuaded Dad to try his hand.

At Norwood Dad cordoned off a space at the bottom of the back garden, making room for not more than four hives. With advice from

Uncle Tim, followed by a diligent reading of *The Scottish Beekeeper* every month, Dad soon became a proficient bee-man. He always wore a hat and veil but he never protected his hands with gloves. 'If you let them crawl over your hands they won't usually sting,' he used to say. If he did get stung, he claimed that it was good for his rheumatism.

Sometimes bee-stings can be dangerous. One summer Aunt Annie, known to the family as Tannie, ever since one of her younger nieces had so named her, was staying with us during her year on leave from India, where she was a medical missionary. Mother was stung on the neck by a bee. Fortunately this swelling subsided fairly quickly. Afterwards Tannie said that if Mother had been in danger of suffocation she would have performed an emergency tracheotomy, using a pen-knife and inserting a narrow tube in her windpipe.

Although after many summers I learned a lot about the bees and their behaviour, I never offered to help Dad except when the time came to extract the honey in the autumn. Dad had bought an extractor and a ripener. The extractor was great fun; firstly, the wax cappings, with which the bees sealed every comb, had to be sliced off. Dad would bring these to the tea-table, dripping with honey, where we would spread them on bread and butter. The wax of the cappings was made by the bees, unlike the cells themselves which were drawn out by the bees from a flat manufactured 'comb' and would not have been so good to eat. Placing the shorn combs vertically in a cage in the extractor, which revolved vigorously when a handle was wound, the honey was hurled out by centrifugal force on to the side of the drum and so downwards where it settled. Inevitably, pieces of wax were thrown outwards too, along with parts of dismembered bees which were removed by a filter when honey passed through a tap at the bottom into the ripener. There it stayed until it was time to fill the glass jars with pure honey.

I used to watch from a distance when Dad opened a hive, lifting out the combs covered thickly with bees. While checking that all was well he would look for queen cells, in case there was the danger of the old queen leaving the hive with half the bees. Swarms are good early in the summer because a new colony has time to produce much honey before the coming of winter stops the gathering of nectar.

The English saying is still true:

A swarm in May is worth a load of hay
A swarm in June is worth a silver spoon
But a swarm in July isn't worth a fly.

The Germans had the same belief:

Wenn in Mai die Bienen schwärmen
So soll man vor Freude lärmen
(When the bees swarm in May then one must shout with joy)

When the bees swarmed, we hoped that they would settle in some nearby accessible place such as the bough of a tree. I remember on more than one occasion coming back from school for the midday meal. 'The bees are swarming, Jim,' said Mother. 'I've telephoned Dad and he's coming home as soon as he can.' We would then go into the garden creating as much noise as possible with sauce-pans and spoons, hoping that the bees, hearing this clamour, would settle quickly on a tree, hanging from a limb in one solid bunch of thousands of bees. When Dad arrived he would shake the bunch into a straw 'skep' where they would remain until he could produce a new hive for them. Sometimes, unluckily, the swarm would fly away too far to be found. One day Mother telephoned Dad at work in Hull to say that a swarm had settled and was hanging from a branch of the Victoria plum tree. Dad could not leave the Customs office, so he explained exactly what she should do. Mother bravely donned Dad's hat and veil and a stout pair of gardening gloves. When Dad came home he found a skep full of bees ready to transfer to a hive.

There were occasions when Dad required a new queen to reign over a colony whose queen had died. From an advertisement in *The Scottish Beekeeper* he would order a new queen. She would arrive by post in a small wooden container with a perforated zinc cover to give air, with a dozen or so royal attendants and food to last the short journey by mail. One imported queen produced a colony of vicious, bad-tempered bees that were difficult to handle.

One summer in the mid-1920s Dad had the idea of moving a couple of hives to the North Yorkshire moors, hoping that they would produce a good crop of heather honey. Having found a site there with the help of a friendly farmer, Dad prepared the bees for their move. He closed the small entrance hole on each hive when all the bees had finished their day's work. Early next morning, before the bees were up, the hives were loaded on to an open motor lorry which Dad had hired. Dad, taking a day off work, travelled with the driver to the moors, some forty miles away. As the driver was helping Dad to lift the hives aboard, one section of a hive slipped, releasing a handful of bees. The last view we had was of Dad sitting on the back of the departing lorry, clapping his hands to kill the few bees which had escaped.

After three months he brought the bees home again. The heather honey with its distinctive flavour was his reward at the end of this adventure. He never repeated the experiment. Instead, he set up several more hives in the orchard of a friendly neighbour where the bees could gather the nectar from trees close at hand.

We often laughed at the ignorance of people generally about the bees and their lives. When one bee crawled across the table when we were having tea in the garden, a visitor asked: 'Do you have names for each of the bees?' 'Yes,' Dad replied promptly, pointing to the bee, 'that one is Habakkuk.'

What fascinated me was that in a colony of bees they all had their duties, from those who looked after the queen to the lowly ones who kept the hive clean. I could never understand the role of the drones in a hive, except that only one of them impregnated the queen on her nuptial flight. The rest of them had no obvious function and were killed off by the bees. If one tapped on the sloping board leading to the entrance to the hive after the bees had retired for the night, a lone sentry would appear. Seeing nothing to be worried about he would retire. Unfortunately, some birds had learned this trick and the lone sentinel was gobbled up as soon as he appeared.

When a beekeeper died it used to be the custom for the remaining spouse to tell the bees. When Dad died many years later in the Cotswolds, where he had retired, he still had several hives in a neighbour's orchard. I do not know whether my Mother remembered to tell the bees that he had died; but my sister Betty told them. The local postman's young son, keen on beekeeping, who had asked Dad for advice, became the owner of the bees, their hives, the extractor and all the other equipment, which Mother gave him.

FIRE ! FIRE !

Who knows how many fires destroyed houses and other buildings in Beverley through the centuries? A great fire seriously damaged the Minster in 1188; the Dominican Friary near Eastgate burned down in 1449 and in 1566-7 eighty houses in Newbegin were destroyed. Nowadays we expect the fire brigade to arrive within minutes of receiving a call, but, before 1924, Beverlonians depended on a volunteer group of men, with hoses connected to the water main. Their hand-cart, with ladders for rescuing people trapped in upper rooms, also carried the hoses. In earlier days, before mains water covered the whole of Beverley, hand-pumps operated by six or more strong men, were in use. A large tank of water was carried, which neighbours would top up with buckets of water from wells or pumps. In the seventeenth century equipment of this kind was provided in various places in the town; in the 1690s the constables were ordered to keep all wells and pumps in Beverley in good repair as a precaution against fire.

I do not ever remember seeing a horse-drawn fire-engine in Beverley; nor did we have a steam-driven engine as used in many boroughs, which produced jets of water far more powerful than the old manual pumps operated by muscle-power. The fire-cart with its equipment used to lean against the wall on the left of the Guildhall at Beverley. It was not until 1924, when the gleaming, powerful motor fire-engine arrived that fire-fighting in Beverley became more efficient. It was housed at first in a station made from unused police cells near the Guildhall. Even then there was not enough money to maintain a full-time brigade; instead, a group of volunteers was recruited. These men had full-time jobs, but had permission from their bosses to down tools when summoned for fire duties. The summons was the firing of a rocket at the Police Station; at that time it was always called a maroon.

When they heard the maroon, the men would dash down on their bicycles, one by one from all directions, to Register Square, where, nearby, the fire-engine was lodged. Seizing their helmets and uniform, they would leap on board the engine. Several times during school holidays, on hearing the maroon, I would race down on my bike to see the fire-engine depart. On one occasion a volunteer fireman arrived on his bicycle just as the engine was moving off. He threw his bike on the pavement outside the Post Office and leapt on board. The crowd of sightseers gave him a rousing cheer.

Then with other boys who had also arrived, we would cycle as fast as we could in pursuit, through the town and out into the country, where the engine threw up clouds of dust. Usually a farmer had called the brigade by telephone when one of his haystacks had caught fire. The fire-engine easily outpaced the following gang of cyclists, but we followed behind until we saw smoke on the horizon. My brother David once joined the pursuit; as the fire-engine roared up Norwood, a fireman's helmet suddenly fell into the road. David picked it up, later handing it in at the police station.

A stack fire at one farm near Cherry Burton threatened some stables. By the time we arrived all the horses had been led to safety; but there remained in the stable many bales of hay. The firemen urged us to join in the job of removing them to safety and this we gladly did.

When all was safe and the fire extinguished, I cycled home, hot, thirsty and smoky after an exciting and memorable day.

SILENTS AND TALKIES

My first visit to the cinema was when my brother David took me to see a Tarzan film. This was probably an episode of the serial *Son of Tarzan* (1920). This was the first of many dozens of visits to see the silent films of the 1920s. We didn't call them silent films, of course, until the coming of the 'talkies' in 1928. Nor did we talk about going to the cinema or to the movies. To us it was always 'going to the pictures.'

Most of my earliest visits to the pictures in Beverley were with my inseparable cousin Geoff. Mutt and Jeff, his older brother Bernard called us, after the two American comic-strip characters. Saturday afternoons were special days for us because Marble Arch in Butcher Row, one of Beverley's two cinemas at that time, had matinées for children. Geoff and I would arrive in good time, clutching our sixpenny pieces for seats in the gallery. In exchange for our sixpence we were given a metal token; with this in hand we raced up the carpeted stairs, handing the token to a young woman at the top. As the lights finally dimmed there was a tremendous roar from the boys and girls below. For fourpence you could sit down below where the children yelled their heads off and sometimes started fighting. The uniformed attendant tried to keep them in order by shouting like a sergeant-major and blowing a referee's whistle. At times he would spray the audience with a mist of perfumed water, the smell of which reached the gallery.

The films were not truly silent, for sound was provided by a pianist, who matched the action on the screen with appropriate music, stirring when horses were galloping across the screen in some Western drama, with tender melodies for the love scenes and sombre music for the sad moments.

Every programme included a serial, a newsreel, a cartoon and sometimes a short travel film. Then came the main picture. Of the cartoons in the 1920s we enjoyed best of all the adventures of Felix, the cat who could never be defeated. Created by an Australian, Pat Sullivan, who had settled in the U.S.A., Felix was the best known and the most popular of all cartoon characters. A rival cartoonist was Max Fleischer, an Austrian in America, who made the inkwell cartoons. Each episode began with a shot of the artist's hand dipping a pen into a bottle of black ink. The figure, which he drew on white paper, started moving. Two of the characters he created were Betty Boop and Popeye the Sailor. Walt Disney's Mickey Mouse followed soon afterwards, with Mickey's voice spoken by Disney himself in the early cartoons.

Each week we watched a thrilling serial. The famous Pearl White, 'Queen of the Silent Serials', was before our time, but my sister Jean remembers being taken by our brother David to see that intrepid lady week after week. The serial I remember was about a man named 'Hutch,' who single-handed defeated his enemies weekly. 'Go get'em Hutch' was always in trouble. One episode left him swimming under the ice in a lake, desperately seeking a hole through which to escape. **SEE NEXT WEEK'S THRILLING INSTALMENT!** were the words printed on the screen at the end. Hutch always escaped to live through another adventure.

Tom Mix, the greatest of all the cowboys, with his wonderful horse Tony, was a great favourite with us; his dog Duke, the Great Dane, appeared in many of the western films he made. Tom was the great hero who always defeated the villains; in hundreds of films he and Tony won the day. How we wished we had horses to ride on the Westwood, shooting all the evil cowboys with our Winchester repeaters or lassoing them with our lariats.

Most of the silent feature films we watched on those happy Saturday afternoons at the Marble Arch were the epic films such as *Robin Hood*, with the athletic Douglas Fairbanks as Robin and Wallace Beery as Richard the Lion-heart. Fairbanks we saw again in *The Thief of Baghdad,* which reminded me of *The 1001 Nights,* which I had been reading by flashlight under the bed-clothes. Wallace Beery played the part of Richard I again in *Richard the Lion-Hearted,* based on the novel *The Talisman* by Sir Walter Scott.

Ben Hur was one of America's biggest epics, in which the battle at sea and the chariot race were unforgettable. Based on a novel by Lew Wallace, the charismatic Ramon Novarro was the long-suffering hero. Next came two grandiose Cecil B. de Mille films: *The Ten Commandments* and *King of Kings*. For the latter, which was a life of Jesus, the Marble Arch hired a small orchestra in addition to the usual piano, which was thought to be inadequate to accompany such an important film. What pleased cousin Geoff was that his brother Bernard was playing the piano. Jesus was played by the veteran English actor H. B. Warner, who appeared in many American films.

The Covered Wagon, another epic film showing how the pioneer settlers moved west across America, was shown at the Picture Playhouse. Paddy Burden decided that such an important historical film should be seen by all the boys at the Grammar School. I cannot remember whether we had to pay, but I remember most of the school crowding into the cinema one afternoon. The Picture Playhouse, Beverley's second cinema, housed in the old Corn Exchange, is claimed to be the oldest cinema in Great Britain. It was certainly the cosiest, with double seats for young lovers. Mr Symonds, the proprietor, was a pioneer cinema manager. With his cine-camera he filmed local events in Hull, Beverley and district, showing them later on the screen as an extra newsreel.

Best of all the films of the 1920s for me was Charlie Chaplin's *The Gold Rush*. From the first sequence, showing the prospectors climbing the snow-covered mountain on their way to the gold fields, to the last frame, I was entranced. For me it was the perfect film, to be seen again and again in later years. Geoff and I had already seen many Chaplin two-reelers, such as *The Cure* and *Easy Street*. We had also laughed our way through many of the adventures of comedians such as Harry Langdon, Buster Keaton and Charlie Chase. Harold Lloyd had entertained us with his death-defying exploits on the tops of skyscrapers. Last, but not least, were the Laurel and Hardy films.

We saw several serious films about the Great War such as *Ypres*, but more to our juvenile tastes were the humorous films such as Chaplin's *Shoulder Arms,* in which Charlie captured both 'Little Willie,' the Crown Prince, and the Kaiser himself. *Alf's Button* from a story by W. A. Darlington told how Private Alf Higgins (Leslie Henson) found that a replacement uniform had one brass button which turned out to have been made from a portion of Aladdin's lamp, which had been melted down for the war effort. On cleaning his button Alf was confronted by Aladdin's genie, the Slave of the Lamp, ready to grant his wishes. The background of Darlington's book was authentic for he had served in the trenches. His story of Alf's subsequent adventures with his friend Bill was ideal material for a film.

The 'talkies' began to take wing about the time I left school in 1930; in fact, some of the best of the early sound films appeared in that year, such as *The Dawn Patrol* in which Richard Barthelmess and Douglas Fairbanks Junior played the parts of two aviators in the Great War. *All Quiet on the Western Front*, based on the best-selling novel by Eric Maria Remarque, was the greatest of all the war films, with Lew Ayres as the young German soldier. *The Rogue Song*, based on the operetta *Gypsy Love* by Franz Lehàr, with Lawrence Tibbett playing the leading part, included Laurel and Hardy in minor roles. *In Gay Madrid* and *Call of the Flesh* also appeared in 1930, both featuring Ramon Novarro and a delightful new actress, Dorothy Jordan, with whom I immediately fell in love; she had already appeared, also with Novarro, in another film *Devil-may-care* (1929), a film about a young soldier in Napoleon's army who falls in love with a girl from an old Royalist family. Also that year appeared *The Desert Song*, based on the musical by Sigmund Romberg and Oscar Hammerstein II. Although crude in parts, the songs were memorable, especially those sung by Carlotta King. These and many more of the early talkies drew me and some of my school friends to the cinemas like a magnet.

Films other than those of British and American origin were rarely shown in Beverley. One exception was the German film *The Blue Angel* (1930), with the legendary Marlene Dietrich and Emil Jannings. Based on Heinrich Mann's novel *Professor Unrath*, it was directed by Josef von Sternberg, who made it in German and English. Marlene's song in the film, *Falling in Love Again,* became so popular that she was still being asked to sing it in her old age.

The French director René Clair's film *Sous les toits de Paris* appeared at the end of the 1920s. It was one of the few foreign films that had a general showing. Although the plot, about a Paris street singer who falls in love, is slender, it became a classic of its kind, with catchy songs and sunny outlook.

So ended a remarkable decade in the history of the cinema. Perhaps if I had studied more at home and gone to the pictures less, I might have obtained better results at school. On the other hand, I would have missed all those silent classics and the remarkable films of the late 1920s and early 1930s when sound came.

BRIDLINGTON

I cannot understand why the prospect of the annual fortnight in September at Bridlington filled me with such ecstasy. For to tell the truth I hated the sea and feared it. But a holiday at Brid, by which name this seaside town is known in Yorkshire, was so different from the routine life of school and home that the smell of the sea, the cry of the seagulls and the everlasting sound of the waves breaking on the shore produced this feeling of bliss.

We children knew nothing of the annual preparations for the holiday: the booking of seaside digs in good time, the sorting out of clothes and all the equipment we would need. All was ready on the day; with some of us and all the luggage piled into Mr Camm's cab, his horse must have realised that there was an extra load, even though Dad and David walked to the station. Finally we were on the platform at Beverley Station, waiting with impatience and a feeling of great excitement for the arrival of the train from Hull which would take us to Brid.

We all knew Robert Louis Stevenson's poem *From a Railway Carriage* from his book: *A Child's Garden of Verses*:

> *Faster than fairies, faster than witches,*
> *Bridges and houses, hedges and ditches;*
> *And charging along like troops in a battle,*
> *All through the meadows the horses and cattle:*
> *All of the sights of the hill and the plain*
> *Fly as thick as driving rain;*
> *And ever again, in the wink of an eye,*
> *Painted stations whistle by.*

As the train neared Brid, each of us was on tiptoe, anxious to be the one who saw the sea first. At Brid station most of the horse-drawn cabs were roofless. We all climbed in, with the luggage, which included the tent and Dad's old army valise, of enormous capacity, which rolled up in the shape of a vast Swiss roll.

Every year we occupied the same space on the beach of the North Shore, against the sea-wall. Dad had made a collapsible square tent

Top left: Jimmy with Joan Smith and her brother and Nannie.

Top right: Jean and Jimmy at Bridlington, about 1921.

David, Jimmy, Jean with Betty, Geoff, Cousins Vera, Peggy and Dorothy at Bridlington, 1921.

covered with stout material which was carried to Brid each year. Our neighbours on the beach for several years were a family with children about our age, accompanied by a jolly nanny who loved to organise games for us children. Mr Smith was a man of wealth, the boss of a lemonade and mineral water factory in the West Riding. One of the daughters, a pretty young girl with bobbed hair, was about my age. Her name was Joan. Another neighbour was the Peabody family; Mr Peabody had a gent's outfitter's shop in Beverley and was a member of the Baptist Church, so we knew them well. Eric, the older son, was about David's age, Ken about Jean's age and Kitty, their sprightly daughter, was a little older than I.

There was always plenty to see and things to do on the beach. From the promenade above the sea-wall you could look down on the wonderful work of a sand-artist. Every day, soon after the tide had receded from the sea-wall, he would stake out a rectangle of virgin smooth sand below the promenade. Barefooted and with only one arm he would each day produce amazing and colourful pictures for the delight of the holiday-makers passing by. His cap, open in the corner of his picture, invited the throwing of pennies or even silver money. He would never fail to look up and say thank you. When he had gone home, leaving his wonderful pictures to the incoming tide, Jean and I used to dig with our spades near where his cap had been. Sometimes we found a few pennies or halfpenny pieces. We threw them back to him the next day; but one day we put one of the pennies in a slot-machine, hoping to get a bar of chocolate. To our dismay, out came two cigarettes wrapped in a small carton. Jean gave them to a young man at our digs who was a smoker.

My sister Jean had always been good at drawing and painting. On one occasion, *The Daily Mail* organised a children's sand-artist competition. Each competitor had perhaps a couple of square yards of the beach allocated. The rule was that only material found on the beach could be used by the competitors, who had to caption their pictures with the words 'Daily Mail, record sale, nearly one million.' Jean was keen to enter and Dad suggested that she should draw one of her Red Indians in profile, entitled 'The Big Chief.' For a head-dress Jean collected a variety of birds' feathers found on the beach. With coloured pebbles and glass for ornaments and powdered brick for the face she produced an interesting chieftain whose long hair was made of seaweed. The judges came along after three hours and Jean, to her delight, won the second prize, which was a spanking new tennis-racket, complete with wooden press. Jean was pleased with it and not envious of the child who had won the first prize. She had overheard one of the judges muttering to his fellow judge. 'Pity about the spelling; but for that she would have been first.' Jean had spelled nearly *nearley*.

Jean and I were lucky one morning, very early, when we were strolling along the beach looking for jetsam. Suddenly Jean spotted a couple of pennies and a little further on a purse which had obviously been in the sea a long time. There were no marks of ownership. The total sum of money was three shillings and fourpence, enough to buy forty penny ice-cream cornets! Dad said we could keep it and because it had obviously been in the sea a long time, there was no need to hand it in to the police.

For me, the main attraction on the beach was the Punch and Judy show. I would stand for hours watching it, until I knew the dialogue by heart. The Punch and Judy man at Brid had a real dog sitting on a shelf which would snarl at Mr Punch when he poked it with his stick. I took great delight in imitating the raucous voice of Mr Punch.

The donkeys fascinated me too. As soon as I heard the tinkling bells on their collars as they trotted down through a tunnel to the beach, I would dash along to be with them. It wasn't that I wanted to ride them; it was just that I liked to be in their presence. The donkey man soon got to know me and he would let me lead a donkey walking when a small nervous child was having a ride. He also had a pony and trap in which people could ride when it was time to return to their digs. Somebody had to go with them to bring the pony and trap back; one day, when his regular assistant was busy elsewhere, he asked me to take a woman and her little daughter back home in a trap. They wished to go slowly so I walked through the town, holding the bridle. On arrival, the lady pressed a shilling into my hand. I gleefully drove the trap back to the beach.

One of the most interesting shows took place outside the harbour wall in the evening at high tide, when a champion swimmer performed amazing aquatic feats for the entertainment of crowds of people on the pier. This muscular man was intrepid; he would stand on the sea-wall calling out loudly: 'Imitation of a porpoise.' Then, diving into the sea, he would swim underwater, coming up for air from time to time, porpoise-fashion. But his most spectacular trick was to have himself chained up by members of the audience and placed in a canvas sack, which was then padlocked. This package was then thrown into the water. The spectators became more restless as time went by, everybody scanning the water, with no sign of the sack. Then, at last, when most of us began to fear that he would never appear again, suddenly he shot to the surface, waving the sacking in the air. After such incredible Houdini-like feats he deserved the cash reward collected in a hat by his assistant from the crowd of watchers on the pier.

It was the custom in some seaside digs for the guests to buy their food, which was then cooked by the landlady. This system seemed to work well, for Mother knew the food we liked. Mrs Boyce, at whose house we stayed year after year, was an excellent cook. One day Dad took my older brother David and me fishing before breakfast; it was not an experience that I wished to repeat. The smell of the petrol on the motor boat combined with the rocking of the boat made me feel queasy. I wasn't actually sick, but as Dad said later: 'He was beginning to look a little green about the gills.' We and the other fifteen or so fishers had lines or rods. We didn't have much luck. I caught a small mackerel on my line, not big enough to take back to the digs.

The icecream stall on the beach was a magnet. To enter it the owner had to duck under the circular counter. The icecream was good and wholesome, probably made by the owner himself and not contaminated with fancy flavourings and colours. One day the owner had left the store, probably to spend a penny. Mother, seeing a small crowd of youngsters and adults waiting impatiently for icecream, suddenly said: 'I'll go and serve them.' We all protested, thinking that the owner would be very angry. Mother soon dispersed the crowd, serving penny cornets and twopenny wafers as she piled up the pennies and sixpences on the counter. The astonished proprietor, to our surprise, thanked her warmly. I don't remember whether he gave her a free icecream, but she certainly deserved one.

Most of our holidays in the 1920s were in Brid, but one year we all went to Whitby. Who can ever forget climbing the 199 steps up to the old abbey there, although some of us maintained that it was two hundred. Another year, in 1919, the year Dad returned from the Great War, we were at Filey, where Jean and I played at running a hospital for wounded soldiers, putting bandages on Jean's dolls. In the course of our medical activities, we accidentally tipped our baby sister Betty out of her pram; but she was well wrapped up and came to no harm. In the streets we saw many wounded soldiers in hospital blue clothes.

Dad could not always take his annual leave from the Customs in Hull in September because his colleagues had to take turns in fixing the dates of their holidays. When he was unlucky, having failed to secure a September date, Dad used to come straight from work to Brid on the train, spend the evening with us and return to Hull on a fast train in the morning.

Brother David and Jean were good swimmers; for them plunges into the sea several times a day were the great delights of the holiday. For me, the cold body-clinging bathing costume (for they didn't have trunks in those days) was to be avoided when possible; but I enjoyed paddling. One morning, however, when most of the children were in the sea, Mr Smith, our neighbour on the beach, offered me sixpence if I would plunge into the sea without stopping. The lure of gold won; after all, it was a whole week's pocket-money. I plunged in and quickly came out again. Old snapshots taken at the time and the professional photos taken by the Snaps man who used to roam the beach show me

The one-armed sand-artist, about 1924.

The Floral Hall, Bridlington, 1923.

wearing my school cap and often a collar and tie, even when it was sunny.

One afternoon I was unhappy. I had a gnawing toothache, probably brought on by eating too much Bridlington rock, the pink variety with the town's name revealed at every bite. So miserable was I that I had retired behind the tent where I sat against the sea-wall in my misery. Suddenly a small ten-year-old found me there. It was Joan Smith, the lemonade manufacturer's daughter. With a look expressing sorrow at my sad plight, she gently kissed me and left without saying a word.

FIRE AT THE FLORAL HALL

Two excitements in one day! For a nine-year-old this was bliss. The first one was that we were going on summer holiday to Bridlington; even the train journey was exciting, from the time the enormous steam locomotive panted its steam and smoke up to the roof of Beverley Station, to the arrival at Brid and the first glimpse of the sea.

We had arrived at Brid station during the morning of Saturday, the 25th of August 1923. After a midday meal at the digs, the family trooped down to the beach, carrying between us the collapsible tent, the towels, bathing costumes, buckets and spades and all the other items needed for an afternoon on the sands.

It wasn't long before the second excitement of the day arrived. Everybody on the beach suddenly saw a great cloud of smoke overhead coming from the town. The Floral Hall was on fire! The beach quickly emptied as the holidaymakers climbed the steps up to the promenade to see what had happened. A more combustible building could hardly have been found. The Floral Hall, close to the seafront, was used mainly for variety shows and concerts. It was built of wood with a tarred roof covering its single storey. The flames had burst through the roof, despite the efforts of the firemen who had already arrived. Dad guided us back to our lodgings, which were less than two hundred yards from the fire. There, climbing on to a nearby wall, David, Jean and I had a clear view of the blazing building. Another fire-engine, drawn by snorting horses, arrived with clanging bell, probably from the nearby town of Filey. In the street was a tangle of hose-pipes as the firemen battled on. The police were there too, keeping back the crowds of people at a safe distance.

It was the first fire I had ever seen and to me, thoughtless of the hardships of those who had escaped, it was magical and a little frightening. I could now boast that I had seen the Floral Hall in flames, that I was there when it happened.

Luckily, there were no casualties; all those taking part in the afternoon variety show had escaped, some with only the clothes they were wearing on stage. We could see some of the young girls, still in make-up and in tears, bewildered at the speed with which the building was reduced to a tangle of charred timbers. The smell of smoke and burnt tar remained for days.

A poster nearby announced that the British comedian George Robey, 'the Prime Minister of Mirth,' was to appear at the Floral Hall the following day. But the next day there was little mirth in Brid. Among the ruins a large tarpaulin had been suspended above the blackened timbers close by the pavement. A notice asked passers-by to contribute to a fund to aid the artistes who had lost all their clothes and belongings. Already this unusual money-box was full of coppers, silver threepenny-bits, sixpences and other silver coins. Almost everybody passing by threw at least a copper or two.

In place of the Floral Hall, which had given pleasure to many, there is now a car park, which replaced the tennis-courts which my sister Betty remembers playing on in the 1930s.

CHRISTIAN WILKIE THIRSK (DAD)

In most households the father looms large in the upbringing of the children. In our family this was not so: Dad volunteered to join the army soon after the Great War began on August 4th 1914. David and Jean, my brother and sister, were old enough to remember him during the next five years, but I was little more than two months old when he left. Although he came home occasionally, either on leave, or after treatment in hospital for a leg wound in 1916, I did not know what it was to have a father until he was demobilised in 1919.

When he came home for good, I alone in the family was not pleased. I had heard much talk of him and I even spoke of 'a Daddy in the France.' But when the real one arrived my little world was turned upside down; it was disrupted also by the arrival of a baby sister. It took many years for me to be reconciled to this large man who took up so much space in the house. For the first few years after the war Dad and I were not on the same wave-length; for the first year or two I did not even believe that he had any authority over me, so accustomed had I become to accepting Mother's decisions. But in the later 1920s, largely because of Mother's understanding of the problem, tensions eased.

Dad's own journey through childhood and youth was not a happy one, without either mother or father. He had been sent to Scotland from Beverley in Yorkshire at the age of five, and his Scottish mother

Lt-Qm C. W. Thirsk, Northants Regiment

died soon after. He was brought up by an uncle and aunt in the little town of Newburgh, Fife, on the banks of the River Tay; his father, being over sixty, was unable to cope with him and his brothers and sister. His uncle, James Wilkie Wood, had a printing business combined with a newsagency and post office. Dad loved his uncle and he, having no children, loved Dad. But his Aunt lavished all her love on Margaret, his little sister, who had been taken into their home along with Dad.

When his uncle died, Dad had reached his teens. As soon as he left the village school he was determined to leave Newburgh and to make his own way in the world. Having some knowledge of post office work, he applied for a job in the main post office at Edinburgh. Work there brought him in contact with an outside world far different from the little town he had left. His first job was in the parcels department; there he quickly learnt most of the place-names of Scotland and knew in which counties they were located. Promotion to the telegraphy section followed. Telegrams at that time travelled along the telephone lines by Morse code. Dad worked shifts and often had to work all night. At the time of the Boer War, lines were busy throughout the night with the newspaper dispatches carrying the latest war news. Dad had already joined the Royal Scots regiment as a Territorial soldier; he told me once that if the war had continued another year he would have been called up to serve in Africa.

After a time he became restless. Seeing a government advertisement announcing a forthcoming examination for entrance to the Customs and Excise service, Dad applied and was successful. His first posting was to London, where he served in the preventive section; this involved boarding and searching ships from all over the world arriving at the Port of London. Salaries were low and Dad had little left when he had paid the landlady for his board and lodging in Islington. Luck came his way when he was posted to Hull; for Dad was already courting my mother, a Beverley girl, whose sister had already married his brother Jim. At Hull the work was mainly in a Customs Office on the ground floor of one of the large bonded warehouses at the side of the old Queen's Dock. In this office Dad spent the next thirty-four years except for five years in the army during the Great War.

From time to time, usually when Mother took us to Hull on a shopping trip, we called at the Customs Office. The tall warehouses were gloomy Victorian buildings; they might even have been pre-Victorian, for Queen's Dock, the oldest dock in Hull, was built in 1778. Behind the Customs Office, and on many floors above, stood enormous casks of wines and spirits from France and other European countries. The smell of wine hung over the building constantly and even entered the office where Dad worked with the other Customs men. I remember a genial foreman employed by the wine merchant, who took me on a tour of the building, showing me how they hoisted the casks to the top of the building from the horse-drawn lorries below. He also let me try my hand at using the machine for putting corks in the bottles. Every pint of wine entering or leaving the building had to be checked by the Customs men.

Soon after the Great War Dad decided to take an examination which would promote him to the rank of surveyor in the Customs. With one of his colleagues they began studying together. Mr Morris, a single man, his wife having died while he was in France in the army, came to our house frequently in the early 1920s. Together they would retire to an attic and test each other on a subject of the syllabus. The day of the written examination at Liverpool came. They travelled there the night before. The next morning, as they were sitting at their desks waiting for the examination papers, Dad saw that Mr Morris was ill. He helped him from the room, and, leaving him with one of the staff who promised to call a doctor, he returned to his desk. Dad did his best to concentrate, but he was worried all morning about Mr Morris, who recovered but was unable to take the examination. When the results were published Dad came seventieth out of those who had sat the examination. Only sixty surveyors were required that year, so he had failed to achieve promotion. The set-back was harder to bear because he knew that in most years seventy or eighty of the top candidates were chosen. The promotion would have meant a higher salary and almost certainly a move to another part of the country.

Dad had dreams that if he had become a surveyor he might have gone back to the Scotland he loved. That would have meant that all of us would have gone to Scottish schools, which at that time were considered better than most schools in England. So we all might have acquired Scottish accents; we would certainly have led very different lives. Although he was disappointed that he had not become a surveyor, he reconciled himself to working in the Customs Office by Queen's Dock. Reading and beekeeping were his main hobbies, but secretarial work at the Baptist chapel, and writing sermons which, as a lay preacher, he delivered at villages near Beverley, took up some of his time.

Although Dad had missed the chance of promotion he had a safe job through the 1920s and in the great depression of the thirties. He was sad when the Second World War came, knowing that all the sacrifices and deaths of his comrades in the Great War had been in vain.

CLARA THIRSK

(One of the Chapman girls)

Had it not been for the skill of the surgeon who saved my Mother's life, neither I, nor my brother and two sisters, would ever have seen this world. Mother had to have her appendix removed in 1905 at the age of twenty-three. The operation was fairly new and had received much publicity when King Edward VII had his removed and had to postpone his coronation until he recovered.

At the time of her illness my Mother was a nanny looking after the four little girls of Mr and Mrs Jameson, who lived in some splendour at Aston Hall, in the village of North Ferriby in East Yorkshire. Mr Jameson was a wealthy timber importer in nearby Hull. The daughters and an older son, who was away at prep school during term time, all loved Mother, and, at seventeen, her age when she was first employed, she was young enough to form a happy relationship with them and the other servants. One of her particular friends was Lizzie Beacock, the head cook, who gave Mother many of the recipes which she used in later life.

Mother enjoyed her eight years at Aston Hall. A holiday in Wales with the family was an annual event. On these occasions special coaches and wagons would be hitched onto the train coming from Hull. Not only the family climbed on board. A coachman with horse and carriage were loaded on the train. How excited the children would be when the great day of the holiday arrived!

The blow fell in 1905 when Mother began to have severe pains. For some days the local doctor administered laudanum, but, when the pain continued, Mr Jameson took her to the Hull Royal Infirmary. Appendicitis was diagnosed and the surgeon

Mother and son (Clara and Jimmy), 1928.

decided to operate immediately. As the appendix had already ruptured, the operation was difficult, involving the insertion of drainage tubes. Mother was ordered complete rest on a water-bed for six weeks. She was 23. Gradually she recovered and was eventually able to return to her duties at Aston Hall. While she was in hospital one of her younger sisters, Gertrude, looked after the children. Mr Jameson paid all the hospital charges and the fees of the surgeon. The children rejoiced to see her again.

Mother was already engaged to be married to my father. In hospital she was worried that, because the operation had been so severe, leaving an enormous scar, she would never be able to marry and have children. The surgeon reassured her. 'Wait two years before you marry,' he said, 'and there will be no problems.'

At Ferriby, with her four girls, Mother learned more about child psychology than she could have found in a dozen textbooks on the subject. It was this practical training which enabled her to win the confidence of any strange child she came across who was in trouble. Instinctively children responded to the words with which she diverted their attention from their woes, bringing smiles to tear-stained cheeks. At all times Mother was patient and calm and it was, I think, this approach which pacified unhappy children.

Mother's wedding in 1907 at the age of twenty-five was a splendid spectacle. Mr and Mrs Jameson insisted on sending a carriage and coachman to Beverley, to carry the bride and her father to the Wesleyan Chapel in Toll Gavel. The carriage was loaded with flowers from Aston Hall. After the honeymoon at Knaresborough Mother and Dad moved to a rented house in Hull so that Dad, who had been in digs at Beverley, would be nearer his work in the Customs and Excise.

When the Great War came in August 1914 Dad volunteered immediately to join the army. Mother stayed on until the spring but removed to Beverley then because of the Zeppelin raids on Hull. There she was near her mother and father and some of her sisters. Mrs Copeland, a neighbour and old friend, often in later years spoke of her fortitude during the war, looking after three chidren whose father was away for so long.

Moving to a larger house in Norwood, Mother worked hard in the 1920s, bringing up her family and making a happy home for Dad to make up for his five years' absence in France. Dad's income as a civil servant in the Customs was reasonably secure, although once in the 1920s all civil servants had a cut in salary. Because he chose to pay school fees for all four of us, believing that a good education was important, he frequently warned us that money didn't grow on trees. However, we had our summer holiday regularly, usually by the sea at Bridlington, and we never felt in any way deprived.

Mother always had a sunny outlook on life; this, coupled with her unfailing optimism, enabled her to cope with the problems of bringing up a family, especially during the first years after the war. Her older sister Florrie was once heard to say: 'You can't *down* our Clara.' She was good at providing meals at short notice. We enjoyed her meat pies, the puddings and the fruit pies. An exception was her batter pudding with rhubarb, which Dad abhorred so much that he called it shudder pudding. Like all her sisters Mother was an expert when it came to making Yorkshire pudding, even though she was born in Lincolnshire. Mother always made her own bread. All four of us children came home from school for the mid-day meal which we called dinner. This was the main meal of the day. Mother would provide a hot meal and a pudding to follow. In winter it would be good to come into the house and warm your freezing hands on a jacket potato straight from the oven. Mother must have been busy most of the morning preparing this meal together with other housework. We all arrived at different times, ate our meal and dashed back to school for 2 p.m. After school we would wait until Dad came home from Hull at about 5.45 p.m. for our tea, which was usually of the Yorkshire kind, with something savoury. Dad fortified himself at midday with a meal at the restaurant of the big department store, Hammonds, in Hull, where he would meet Mr Morris and other friends every day.

Mother was a kind and generous woman, always ready to offer help to a neighbour or to anybody in trouble. My sisters say that all their school friends loved coming to our house, for Mother always made them feel welcome. She had little time for any spare-time activity, for she had no idle moments in the day. Her hobby was people and talking to people. None of her seven sisters or two brothers was shy. 'Chapmans for cheek' was a saying often heard in the family. Mother was easy with strangers and would be quickly exchanging life histories with anybody she met on a bus, in a train or anywhere.

Knitting was one activity that she did carry on while talking or on a train journey. The things she mostly made were socks for Dad and for us. Mending clothes and keeping the High School uniforms spick and span was an endless chore. Often when working in the house, cleaning, ironing, cooking or at any time, she would be singing. Her voice was not trained, but she often sang hymns around the house and she knew the well-known ones by heart and always sang in tune. Although no poet, Mother had learnt many English poems at school and could still recite them in her old age. Macaulay's *Lays of Ancient Rome* was her favourite book of poems and she had learnt at school the whole of *How Horatius Kept the Bridge*.

Mother did have some help with the housework. On washdays every Monday a woman came to help. These were the days before washing-machines had arrived. And every Friday another woman, the faithful Mrs Emma Peck, came to clean and polish. She was a widow, struggling to care for her teen-age son. Emma soon became part of our family. She was a great lover of the films and very knowledgeable about the stars of the screen. I often had long discussions with her about the films which were on at the Picture Playhouse. Mrs Peck often slept through two shows because it was warmer there than in her little terrace house in Dyer Lane. She was illiterate and when the time came to draw her old age pension, Dad helped by filling in the forms. When it came to the signature Mrs Peck confessed that she could not write her name. 'I can make a cross,' she said. But that would not do for Dad. He wrote her name on a piece of paper and made her write it again and again until she could sign the application form.

At the end of the 1920s we were all still living at home. David worked in the Midland Bank in Hull; Jean attended the Hull College of Art; I was just about to leave school and look for a job and Betty was still at school. But by 1937 the whole family had left the nest. I went, first, to be a librarian in Lancashire, David moved to a bank in Darlington, Jean was married to a farmer in the West Riding of Yorkshire and Betty went to a secretarial college in London.

Mother walked down one day to Briggs and Powell, the iron-mongers in the Market-Place, to buy a smaller casserole, remarking sadly to the assistant: 'There's only two of us now.'

Dad, Mother, David, Jean, Jimmy, Betty. 1923.